CW01635594

CREATIVITY AND BECOMING

CREATIVITY AND BECOMING

ON ART, WRITING, AND ORTHODOX SPIRITUAL LIFE

JEFF GRAHAM

FOREWORD BY
NICHOLAS SAMARAS

SAINT PATRICK PRESS - CALGARY

Saint Patrick Press, Inc., Calgary T2T 6B7
© 2024 by Saint Patrick Press

All rights reserved. No part of this book may be reproduced in any form or by any electronic or mechanical means without written permission from the publisher, except in the case of brief quotations in articles and reviews.

For more information, write to us:
Saint Patrick Press
P.O.Box 86076
Marda Loop
Calgary, Alberta
T2T 6B7

Second edition
Paperback: ISBN 13: 9781998067060
Name: Jeff Graham.

Title: Creativity and Becoming: On Art, writing, and Orthodox spiritual life.
Description: Second edition. |
Calgary: Saint Patrick Press, 2024. |
Foreword: Nicholas Samaras
Subject: Creativity | Art and Writing | Orthodox Spiritual Life

Check out other titles on our website: saintpatrickpress.com
Read through our blog at saintpatrickpress.com/blog
Mailing list or other queries: info@saintpatrickpress.com
To follow us on X: spatrickpress
To follow us on Instagram: saintpatrickpress

+

I arise today
Through a mighty strength
The invocation of the Trinity
Through belief in the Threeness
Through confession of the Oneness
Of the Creator of all creation . . .

To my wife and children, for their love.

To Nicholas Samaras, for his inspiration.

Akathist of Thanksgiving: Glory to God for All Things

Ikos 7

Through the descent of the Holy Spirit, You enlighten the thought of artists, poets, and scientific geniuses. Through the power of the inmost Mind they are prophetically able to perceive Your laws, opening for us the abyss of Your creative wisdom. Their works involuntarily speak of You. Of how great You are in Your creation; of how great You are in men.

Glory to You for all you have kept hidden in Your Wisdom;
Glory to You for the genius of the human mind;
Glory to You for the life-giving strength of work;
Glory to You for the fiery tongues of inspiration;
Glory to You O God unto ages of ages![1]

CONTENTS

FOREWORD

One can never know how or when a seed is planted. All we can do is create art and let it go into its own life. I have always shared with my students that "poetry books teach you how to feel; poetry criticism books teach you how to think." I would include creativity in this equation. Reading Jeff Graham's *Creativity and Becoming*, I'm enriched by the breadth of this book and the seamless approaches he wields with philosophies and creativity. All philosophies become a consideration of near-divine understanding and the human condition striving to create, endure, and survive whole. If you appreciate depth, this is a great and essential read.

Nicholas Samaras
New York, 2024

INTRODUCTION

My heart is overflowing with a good theme; I recite my composition concerning the King; My tongue is the pen of a ready writer. Psalm 45:1

Pop-Creativity

There are many books written on or about creativity and the creative process. Some of my favourites are Stephen Pressfield's *The War of Art,* Mihail Csikszentmihalyi's *Flow, Steal Like* an Artist by Austin Kleon, and *Daily Rituals* by Mason Currey. One that is particularly robust is Robert Keith Sawyer's *Explaining Creativity: The Science of Human Innovation.* These books and many others like them deal with the creative process as a kind of algorithm—a way of living and working that fosters new ideas and that root out those habits that impede one's ability to be free and spontaneous and dynamic. Creativity in such books is understood as a 'method' that one can learn and improve on and thus grow in one's practice, which may be helpful or fruitful.

However, while worthwhile reading on practical methods for creative work, these books do not provide a way of creativity that corresponds to the simple desire to encounter God in the making of art. The books listed above may talk about 'spirituality' but not about how creativity flows out of the deep spiritual practice that opens us to union with God, our neighbour, and all of creation. In such a way of being, creativity is an epiphenomenon of spiritual practice, of an encounter with God, and not an end in itself. Thus creativity in this more dynamic way comes out of a life that is lived in Love and Joy, and not a problem that must be created and solved. It is thus a mystery that is lived, not a series of algorithms or processes or tools for thinking and systematizing in the 'right' way. Those latter aspects of creativity may be helpful, but the creativity I am writing about here is an ontological way of creating; a way of creating that is a way of being and becoming.

The Creative Process

My first real introduction to creativity as a process was as a consultant. I worked with an architect who was a student of Frank Lloyd Wright. This architect had built a system for facilitating individual and group creativity that led to emergent solutions for complex organizational and even global problems; problems whose complexity would befuddle and overwhelm conventional ways of problem solving within the corporate world. Being trained by this architect, I became part of his small group of international consultants who taught and facilitated companies and NGOs through this rigorous creative process. The peak of our work was with high-profile global think tanks facilitating world leaders to plan out the destiny of humanity and the planet itself. The more I learned and facilitated this process, the more I applied its principles and practices to my writing and overall life. Creativity thus became a set of algorithms or what we called "creative habits".

However, over time I began to see that such methods of creating inflated my ego. And I realized over many years that the way I was creating was literally akin to stealing fire from the gods, or, as Merton describes in his literary writings and elsewhere, "Promethean". There was thus something off with the methods and habits I was employing in my writing and overall work; there was something spiritual about it, some kind of spiritual power I was accessing that I was trying to get a grip or hold of, which, over time, had changed me into someone else—or at least had accentuated and embodied the basest part of myself; that the creative methods I was using and teaching had impinged themselves on me ontologically, and had an impact on my overall being in the world, and thus, somehow, on my very soul.

About ten years later, the architect I had been working with, and whose process I had now become astute in, revealed to me the spiritual source of his ideas—indeed, as he explained, it was a spiritual practice tied into magic and the occult. The timing of that revelation was strange, because over the decade I was his student I was a philosopher, a lover of ideas. I had no need of God, having renounced Him and the Christianity of my upbringing decades prior. I was a *flâneur* in the world of ideas, not committing myself to anything, but being free to explore every whim, every fancy, every intellectual delight. As Martin Heidegger wrote in his essay *Philosophy and Christianity*, I could not commit to Christianity, or any religion for that matter, lest I give up the quest for truth. My life was a pursuit of my passions. But working with this architect, working with world leaders in Switzerland, being led into this world of designing the new age at the highest levels, I fell into chaos and addiction, and reached the end of my life. The choice: death or . . . what?

Over that decade of working with the architect, a friend of mine—an Orthodox Christian—had given me all sorts of Orthodox books to read, and at one time taught me the Jesus Prayer with a prayer rope. Thus in that moment of despair, when death became a clear and efficient option to my pain, I remembered the Jesus Prayer and cried out: "Lord Jesus Christ, Son of the living God, have mercy on me a sinner!" And like the icon of Holy Saturday, I felt a grip on my wrist and a lifting of my spirit into safety, into Life Himself. That was the beginning.

Back to the Architect . . .

The architect and I had a very long meeting one day during which he finally revealed to me that the roots of the system was magic. To go to the next level of my training, he said, I needed to join two secret societies. My gut was right: I had come under the power of something that had tried to drag me down into death. Now, with a renewing Love for Christ, for God, I believe the Holy Spirit opened my eyes to the truth of what I had, under the guise of creativity and design, fallen prey to. I asked question after question, partly stupefied by what I was hearing and partly filling in the blanks of ten years of esotericism, and I was slowly waking up from a kind of spell I had been under. When all was revealed to me — when the esoteric was uncovered—I broke off the relationship, left the consulting work completely, and curled up into a period of seeking God for healing and insight for the next stages of my life. For under that period of time, and all the training and all the practicing, my soul was wounded, and it was wounded at the level of my will and desire and freedom to create. I believe what saved me from the bondage I was in and what gave me the insight to see and flee from all that I was involved in was God. And with the Jesus Prayer uttered that dark night, I had entered a path, a Way, of conversion, which was the initial opening towards Orthodoxy that would culminate eight years later in the waters of baptism. It was also a time of reevaluating what creativity actually is, and how I could learn to create outside of the Promethean, egoistic, or demonic.

The activity of healing and recovery was reflection, prayer, conversations with many people, and reading and listening to anything that would help reframe creativity for me. I needed answers. I had spent a decade of studying and applying many different creative methods, working with very creative people, and using creativity to facilitate world leaders in long-range plans for humanity. But in the course of it all I had become someone I didn't want to become—I was far from becoming myself, and, in fact, didn't even know who I was! The processes I was using were considered 'spiritual' which in my materialistic disenchanted mind was a cliché and not something real. But I realized there were indeed spiritual forces at work, forces that were summoned and leveraged for power and control and insight into the future. Hence, I only really knew creativity as a conduit of the ego, as a way of asserting *my* mark, doing whatever it took to make *my* vision known in the world. I thus needed to know and understand what creativity could possibly mean as light, as something inspired by God. Could God inspire us creatively? How? Again, I needed answers!

Awake on the Lake

It was a warm July night on Lake Couchiching in Ontario. My family and I were staying at my in-law's house. Given the number of family members also staying at the house, my wife, children, and I were sharing a bedroom. I couldn't sleep: maybe it was the mugginess of the evening, the prodding of my son's foot into my back, the gobs of watermelon I had eaten before bed, too much espresso and bonfire smoke —I don't know. Nevertheless I was inspired. When I can't sleep I usually like to read, but in this instance I put on a podcast. It was a poet named Nicholas Samaras who had given a talk at an Orthodox conference on creativity called the Climacus Creativity Conference. I had not heard of Nicholas Samaras, but the talk seemed interesting enough. The title was *Poetry as Spiritual Pilgrimage into Beauty.*

I plugged my headphones in, took a deep breath, shifted my body further away from my son's ever encroaching foot, and listened to Samaras's talk as the filtered moonlight faintly illumined the room. From the moment Samaras began his talk I was drawn into another world, a world of creativity I had never been to before; a truly enchanted world in which spiritual practice and art and creating were one and the same. Before I knew it, I had goosebumps everywhere and was wiping tears from my eyes. While listening to Samaras, I realized I was on my own pilgrimage into Beauty; a movement towards healing as a writer and as a person.

The highlight of Samaras's talk is his story about going to meet Elder Paisios on Mount Athos. The elder greets him and brings him inside his house, makes him something to eat, and talks to him. Samaras shares with him his aspiration to use his creative work, his poetry writing, to enter deeper into God and draw closer to Him. The elder listens and then tells him a parable.

There is a man who seeks to make the purest olive oil, but he can't. Why? Because the olives he has gathered are hard, or bug eaten, or rotten in parts, or flawed in other ways. So what does the farmer do? He cuts out the parts that are hard or bug eaten or rotten and with the parts that are usable he is able to make pure olive oil.

Samaras shares in his talk that by this and subsequent encounters with Elder Paisios, and the latter's parable, his life was changed. And as I laid there in bed with my earbuds still plugged in and tears in my eyes, I was being changed too— the elder's words had reached and inspired me too. And instead of the talk helping me eventually sleep, it kept me up all night. The next morning I was so taken aback by Samaras's talk that I emailed him, asking him to share more with me about how Elder Paisios's story had changed his life. The next day or so, Samaras responded to me, and we had a very rich correspondence. Samaras's 'Pilgrimage into Beauty' and his response to my email—along with other correspondences I had with him —changed my life at a time when I was struggling to understand my calling as a writer, and more importantly how I could live creatively as a Christian.

Over time I began to see that creativity can change one's life —for good or ill. What I read and heard from Samaras was that creativity when authentic comes out of a life, a person, whose heart and mind are attuned to God in an ongoing way; that creativity, art, writing, composing music, the creation of icons flow out of one's pursuit of a loving union with God. And over time I started seeing this pattern in other writers too: Thomas Merton, Henri Nouwen, J.R.R. Tolkien, Alexander Solzhenitsyn, and, albeit more abstractly, the lives of saints.

How to Read this Book

This book is neither a prescription, nor some kind of manual for boosting creativity. It is merely a set of insights and thoughts disparately strung together—what Kierkegaard would probably regard as "crumbs"—in the hopes that one, several, or many will find inspiration somewhere between these pages. In fact I have intentionally avoided giving its chapters any kind of structure or flow, thus to provide a sense of discovery, and even the possibility for divergence. Such a lack of structure will nevertheless facilitate two kinds of readers: 1) those who believe one must read a book in its entirety, cover to cover, and 2) those who like to skim books, dipping in and out of them as their curiosities and whims are piqued. Needless to say, engage the material as it suits you at any given time.

What it's All About

Creativity and Becoming is a compilation of writers and artists, philosophers and saints, who have thought, lived, and written deeply about creativity and spiritual practice. It is written for those who are seeking to create in a way that gives honour and glory to God and to be drawn into loving union with Him.

The leitmotif of this book as it were is this: That when we approach the making of art as a spiritual practice, as a way into or an expression of loving union with God and others, art becomes secondary to the true work of art that is being created—us. Yes, us. We become the work of Art that God wants to create us into, into that authentic self He has created us to be, into icons that reflect His uncreated light. For what purpose? To share that light, as Samaras puts it, as a help and inspiration for others.

Feast of the Holy Cross, 2024

1

CREATING IN A SECULAR AGE

IVAN ILYIN AND THE FOUNDATIONS OF CHRISTIAN CULTURE

The importance of creating Christian culture in the midst of a secular age that is disenchanted and fallen and in need of healing.

Create in me a clean heart, O God; and renew a right spirit within me. . . . The sacrifices of God are a broken spirit; a broken and contrite heart You will not despise. Psalm 51:10, 17

A Contentious Philosopher

Ivan Ilyin has become a contentious Russian philosopher in recent times according to popular media. In 2009—fifty-five years after Ilyin's death—Vladimir Putin had Ilyin's remains moved from Zolikon Switzerland to Russia, and had his grave consecrated. And there have been strange conspiracies written about Ilyin's sway over modern politics, such as the part he had to play in foiling Donald Trump's re-election! Moreover, my blog post, from which this chapter derives, has received a number of fomenting comments from people seething and cursing at me for the gall in honouring someone who is a glorified Russian nationalist.

So with all the strange press and castigation from a few readers, why would I write about Ivan Ilyin in this book about creativity? Because Ilyin's call for the creation of Christian culture, and the social, political, and religious milieu in which he was writing, is as critical for us today as it was a hundred years ago. For in Vladimir Lenin's Russia of the 1920s, people were being cancelled as they are today, particularly those who were Christians, or writers, poets, and artists whose work pointed others beyond the materialism of the Bolsheviks. Such people, according to Lenin and Trotsky, were a danger to freedom, to socialism, and to the movement that would go on to violently overthrow the tsars, the Orthodox Church, and Russian civilization leading to the death of over 60 million people. For those of us living in the chaos of the 21st Century, for those of us who long to create things that point people to God, Beauty, transcendence, the struggles Ilyin and others of his time had are our struggles now too.

The Philosophers' Ship

Ilyin's beliefs about creating Christian culture are elucidated by the Philosophers' Ship. The Philosopher's Ship was a term given to two ships on which many Russian intellectuals were exiled by Vladimir Lenin from Soviet Russia to Germany in 1922. The ships transported more than 200 expelled Russian intellectuals and their families from Petrograd (St Petersburg) to the seaport of Stettin Germany. Ilyin and his wife were on one of those ships, along with Nicholas Berdaeyev and Nikolai Lossky, the latter of whom was the father of Orthodox theologian

Vladimir Lossky. The list of those aboard the Philosophers' Ship was made up of intellectuals and artists who opposed the Bolshevik regime and the scourge of materialism under the fomenting leadership of Vladimir Lenin. These intellectuals, writers, philosophers, artists and religious thinkers were those "who believed in transcendental values, collective knowledge, and communal faith" whose "metaphysical antiquities had no place in Lenin's world which was anti-metaphysical, rationalist, atheist."[1]

In such a regime, "reason took a perverse, political form … which became the foundation of the totalitarian system. It led to a militant and incriminating ban on all expressions of faith and an attempt to destroy individual conscience and human inwardness."[2] Those who were not given the blessing of being thrown out of Russia were instead exiled to the far reaches of Siberia and eventually killed. Such were the victims of Lenin's growing cancel culture. The exiled on the Philosophers' Ship were members of "a mythical tribe from a lost world."[3]

And yet, while Lenin and Trotsky were divesting Russia of the metaphysical through exile and persecution, philosophy in the west had also exiled its mystics and metaphysicians, embracing a movement of analysis whose system was being built on logic and empiricism through the works of Bertrand Russell and other radical empiricist philosophers. Even more 'abstract' continental philosophers of the west, such as Martin Heidegger, had demystified the world as indirect and ironic spokespersons of disenchanted Lutheran Christianity.[4]

The emigres exiled on Lenin's ships thus came to a Europe that too was undergoing great change. The materialist philosophy that had passed like a disease to the shores of

Russia had originated in the Europe they were now banished to. One can only imagine men and women, many of them Orthodox Christians, abandoned to a place where the mystical had been snuffed out centuries prior by the Protestant Reformation, and now the seedbed of atheism, communism, materialism, and Bolshevism. Had not Dostoevsky foreseen this European plague back while writing *The Devils* and *The Brothers Karamazov*? Yet here they were: the mystical tribe who once held high rank in Russian society now cast out and left to assemble in supporters' houses and bereft street corners. But they didn't stop writing and painting and giving lectures and building culture. In fact, creativity and thought flourished in the areas where these emigres were exiled. This is the context in which Ilyin inspires his readers to re-create and reclaim Christian culture.

Foundations of Christian Culture was published in 1938. In that year Ilyin was under surveillance by the Nazis, and financially aided by Sergei Rachmaninoff to abscond to Geneva. Hence, Ilyin was writing about creating Christian culture within a political and social milieu that was profoundly oppressive and destructive to the human spirit. And this came on the heels of the October Revolution of 1917 which Ilyin described as the most terrible catastrophe in the history of Russia. Ilyin was imprisoned for his alleged anti-communist activity before eventually being exiled on the Philosophers' Ship. Ilyin observed that Christianity in the 20th century was under attack across the world through the creation of anti-Christian culture.

> Everything that has occurred in the twentieth century, and continues today, is proof . . . that Christianity in the world is suffering a serious religious crisis . . . There is a wide anti-Christian front that has tried to create an un-

> Christian and anti-Christian culture. This phenomenon is not a new one . . . The process of separating culture from religion, faith, and the Church began a long time ago. In Europe and America, 'secular culture' and secularization itself can trace their beginnings all the way to the Renaissance.[5]

Ilyin traces the dis-ease of culture back to the Renaissance, in which humanity became the centre of the universe—as Protagoras said, "Man is the measure of all things." It signified a shift away from the teachings of the Church as central to the life of the person and a return to a renascence of the ancient Greek way of life, with an emphasis on the sciences, observation, and inductive reasoning, which led to the development of the scientific method and formal logic. The Renaissance was also a time of magic and alchemy, such as in the tireless work of Isaac Newton and many others to discover methods for, among other things, turning base metals to gold; and that it was not just the 'culture' of the ancients that was sought during that time, but their knowledge—and the 'sources' thereof. A disenchanted world seeking re-enchantment. The human as god, and knowledge as the weapon it wields.

A Secular Age

One philosopher that does a marvellous job at painting a fuller, clearer picture of the "religious crisis" that Ilyin was writing about is Charles Taylor, particularly his book *A Secular Age*. In *A Secular Age*, Taylor describes the religious crisis as one through which the world has become 'disenchanted' by an obsession with all forms of empiricism and logical analysis. We no longer believe in a transcendent world that impinges itself on us and exists apart from us; rather as humans we become the centre of all experience and believe only what is somehow validated by our experience. Charles Taylor's book is therefore seminal for anyone interested in understanding the shift from the Christian Age, as it were, to the Secular Age. Part of tracing the course Charles Taylor takes us through is the rise of Bolshevism and the dismantling or attempted dismantling of Christianity in 20th century Russia. As Ilyin writes, "The culture of our time continues this separation from Christianity but not only from Christianity. Contemporary culture is losing its religious spirit, its meaning and its beauty . . . It has left Christianity but wanders the wasteland aimlessly."[6]

The source of this falling away of Christian culture from meaning and beauty is the 'I' that has set itself in place of God. The 'I', the ego, has become God. In such an orientation to the world, God becomes something to merely 'bracket', to put on the shelf, while the 'I' seeks its own scientific breakthroughs, its own power through the 'rite' of political institutions and ceremonies, and ensures every possible need and want is met now if not ten minutes ago.

In the midst of a society going mad with Bolshevism, and the dismantling of all things beautiful and good and true, what is the answer? "Is there a creative way out of this situation?" asks Ilyin. "How can we end it? Is renewal of culture even possible? And how can we bring it about?" Ilyin is saying we must fight back against the attack of culture by becoming people who work and are diligently (re-) creating it in ways that are beautiful and true and good. To bring about this culture, to be culture-shapers and makers, requires first and foremost a renewal of ourselves; a return of our own souls away from a life of ego to a loving union with God and neighbour. If the ethos of modern culture is "do whatever you want," then we need to pursue a life in which we place ourselves fully into the hands of God in relationship. St Pope Kyrillos VI had this beautiful statement: "All I have is Yours." But how do we enter this process of renewal and self-surrender in the midst of raging egoism? Ilyin gives one example, namely the active reading and meditation upon scripture.

> When reading the Holy Scripture, the reader must not simply register what he reads with his mind, but he must try to find and confirm in himself that which is described in the text. . . . He must try to evoke within himself the state of mercy and to dedicate himself to it, to contemplate God's perfection with the heart and to abide in it until the heart and the will (the action of conscience) are filled with it; to find within oneself the power of love and to turn to it (even for a moment) toward God, to mankind, and all that is alive.[7]

Here for Ilyin, the renewal of our lives, of our souls, comes through the active meditation on Holy Scripture. We must read scripture with our hearts (nous), and dwell on it until the heart and the mind are filled with it. But that's not all. The power of the reading then emanates out in love—yes, if even for a moment!—towards God, all of humanity, and, not only that, but to all that is alive, to all creation. This is not a small point.

This renewal is not just interpersonal but cosmic as well. Like the words of Christ in the book of St Mark, "Go into all the world and preach the Gospel to every living creature."[8] The work of this renewal is entering deeper into loving union with God and every living creature, which includes nature itself. Our work must be towards renewal of relationship with God, our neighbour, and all of creation.

The growth of the artist is thus a process of taking off the old man and putting on the new which is the true self who is Christ. And the one who discovers the true divinity of Christ thus becomes transformed by the renewal of the mind. In Orthodoxy we talk about this discovering Christ eucharistically, that is, through the offering of His Body and Blood in the Bread and Wine and us receiving it with open hearts. We thus partake of God into ourselves—body, soul, and spirit—and He heals us and restores us. Hence to create culture first begins with turning the magnifying glass to our hearts and eucharistically growing in loving union with God.

As the ego wears down and we begin to see ourselves and God in a clearer light, our experience of the natural world begins to change too. Nature is not something that exists merely in the mind, but is part of an objective world that impinges itself on us. We stand before the beauty and awe of the natural world, perceive its order, its wonder, its magnitude. We stand in the midst of it as deeply connected to it, as alive in it, as nourished by its air and water, warmed by its fire, edified by its vegetation. And most importantly, as Alexander Schmemann explains, our vocation as artists, as human beings, is to offer the created world back to God in thanksgiving, and, Ilyin would add, art-making.

By creating art, we affirm the Beauty and order of creation. We use created things that become transfigured through our blessing and creating. It is here that we shape the world by offering it back to God and creating with it. Hence, wood and egg yolk and all the materials that make paint become windows into heaven. The paper made from trees become matter on which is provided Holy Scripture, or a way for a reader's heart to be edified by beautiful prose. Wood becomes the stuff of chapels, water the place of encountering Christ in holy baptism, oil the balm of healing. By blessing nature we affirm its reality and offer it back to God through which it is transfigured to its true nature; and, in that process, we too are transfigured.

There is a common caricature of the artist in popular culture: the one who rushes here and there engaging in all matters of hedonism to get the 'right' experiences for his or her art. The artist as re-creator of Christian culture seeks desperately to draw closer to God through the sacraments of the Church; to grow in loving union with God and with all creation. Ilyin:

> Surely Christ Himself accepted the world and was incarnate not to teach us to reject the world, abhor the creation of God, but to show us the true path toward faithful, Christian world acceptance. . . . And whoever accepts the world includes creatively taking on this world as part of life's journey; that is, he assumes the task of the perfecting (completing) of self, neighbour, and matter itself through his spirit. This is also the essence of Christian culture.[9]

To Re-Enchant the World

The direction of the artist as cultural re-creator is—returning to Charles Taylor—to re-enchant the world, to bring it back to its original harmony with God, ourselves, and one another. I think here of J.R.R. Tolkien who wrote to engage the reader not only in good 'moral' narratives about the battle of good and evil and the war against the most evil parts of ourselves, but also to present a true picture, an icon, of the *really* real world: the stuff of elves and dwarfs and magic and angels. Hence the work of the artist is to bring to bear the transcendent world to the spectator. It is to bring meaning and life to what many consider to be ‘crude lifeless matter’. It is to open the spectator to the world as it truly is.

The creation of Christian culture is for everyone. It is a way to offer the world back to God and “give it form through love.” This is a way we can fulfill our role as priests, even if we are considered ‘laypeople’: to offer the world back to God in our prayers, in our labour, and our creativity. Ilyin saw this potential of those Christian philosophers and writers and artists around him to reclaim culture for Beauty, Goodness, and Truth:

> This task cannot be finished by any single age, any single people, any generation, for every age and generation must strive to accomplish this task in their own way, even if that means that they fail in their own way. To become imbued with the spirt of Christ’s teaching and to pour out that spirit into your life and into the physical world—this is our task, and it reveals an immense inner freedom and magnificent creative expanse before us.[10]

And are we not in a similar situation now? Are we not on the brink of the unthinkable? Have we not already seen the total breakdown of civil-ization through global banking elites, powerful NGOs, and the world health regime? Have we not already seen voices cancelled, exiled even, who have sought to uncover and speak the truth in a world gone mad in relativism and falsity? Have we not already seen churches shut down, pastors pulled from their vehicles on highways and dragged to prison? Have we not already seen the downfall of humanity, of civilization to the woke mobs who have no sensitivity to the human experience—oppressed or otherwise—but are merely concerned about taking power and punishing and subjugating certain groups of people, typically those who are also interested in the transcendent and the mystical?

Have we not already witnessed 'Reason' stripped of its dignity and left naked in the howling chaos and brooding darkness of insanity? Is this not the time to reclaim what is Beautiful in a world that celebrates brokenness and death? Is it not the time to create and inspire people, to create culture that feeds their desire, their thirst, for the Transcendent Logos, for Christ Himself and the Beauty of creation? If you can no longer sit back and watch through the attenuated vision of your phone screen the world frothing mad around you without the urge to write something or paint something or start a podcast or a movie production house, then Ivan Ilyin is speaking to you, and this is your moment to join the growing movement of people who seek to recover the Beauty now stolen, to reclaim the Goodness turned heavily on its head, and to affrm the Truth of who Christ is and who we are. Ilyin:

> [We must] accept the world as a consequence of accepting Christ, and to build a Christian culture on top of that edifice. Thus owing from the Spirit of Christ, we may bless the world, not condemning its external forms and laws, not to debilitate its spiritual power, but to overcome it all, transfigure it, and beautifully give it form through love, will, thought, labour, creativity, and inspiration.[11]

Beauty simply Is. For Beauty is the eternal Logos, Christ Himself. And those of us who are filled with Him, who seek after Him through our creative expression, through our work, through our relationships, by inspiring others and being inspired—through all such effort, we are doing the work of Beauty Himself, and thus we are all artists. As

Ilyin writes above, our love for Christ is a love for Beauty; and our working in and through Christ, in the power of the Holy Spirit, is what gives, renews, restores that form, that Beauty to the world. We are more than merely conquerors; we are shapers and restorers of the world that God created and sustains.

And we also do this work in the face of, in the midst of, a world system that is carefully and strategically designed for power and control. One way it controls is through fear and chaos. Just look again at the events of the last decade —how much fear has been used to oppress and control people; how much destabilization through banks and health crises and revolutionary protests and the capricious changes in government, where a criminal can walk out of his prison cell and into the presidency of a country. And now the fomenting mobs, the gangs of crowds driven mad through mass media, are calling for the dismantling of all that is good. What's up is down, and what's down is up.

Everything is up for grabs; for the twenty-first century is a period of upheaval and chaos, of fear and loathing, of definitive winners and losers, of a brutal dialectic, the clash of all clashes, belief without hope of ever being re-synthesized into something true and real. These are the conditions in which we artists are called to do our most important work.

This is how I imagine today's Christian culture to be created—the hearts of people that have already been shaken to their core by the current and coming calamities that have arisen thanks to atheism and anti-Christianity, will begin freely to return to the contemplation of Christ and to the bringing of the gifts of His Spirit back to life and culture. This is our hope as writers and publishers, painters and sculptors, film makers, lawyers, entrepreneurs, parents, and young people: that we bring the message of Christ's everlasting love and comfort to as many as possible. To be light to the world and reflect Beauty in our lives. We can do it through loving others, through offering the world to God in our prayers, and we can do it, indeed, through creating and becoming art.

2

"TO THE LAST WORD!"

DOSTOEVSKY AND THE WRITER'S CONVICTION

Fyodor Dostoevsky shows us what it means to write with prophetic passion. This chapter is a glimpse into how Dostoevsky's "to the last word!" became The Brothers Karamazov.

Lord, who may abide in Your Tabernacle? Who may dwell in Your holy hill? He who walks uprightly, and works righteousness, and speaks the truth in his heart. Psalm 15:1-2

Prefaces Read on Tarmacs

I was sitting on an airplane with a worn out copy of Dostoevsky's *The Devils* in my hand. The plane was still on the tarmac, which is the perfect time to read. Perhaps you're the kind of reader that goes right for chapter one, skipping over any prefaces or prologues. I tend to read the first sentence of the preface and head straight to chapter one, only to return to the front matter of the book halfway through said chapter, and that's exactly what I did on this occasion of reading *The Devils*.

Sometimes front matter can be lacklustre: a simple introduction to the book by the editor or translator, or one that discouragingly sketches out the yawning abyss between the Russian and English translation nothing shy of a brutal murder of the original and a dog's breakfast of a stitch job. But once in a while you read front matter that is actually inspiring, that contains something that you just need to write down somewhere. A nugget that drops into your mind and grooves deeper in. The nugget that forms this chapter offers a glimpse into the creative passion of Dostoevsky shot through with a deep dive into the prophetic.

> "I am thinking of writing a huge novel, titled 'The Atheist'!" [Dostoevsky] wrote from Florence, Italy to his friend Mykov on 23 December 1867, "but before I sit down to write it I shall have to read almost a whole library of atheists, Catholics, and Greek Orthodox theologians."

Dostoevsky had the protagonist worked out only schematically, the providence of which he explains in the following:

> I have the chief character. A Russian of our set, and middle aged, not very educated but not uneducated either, a man of quite good social position who suddenly at his age loses faith in God. . . . His loss of faith in God makes a tremendous impression on him. . . . He pokes his nose among the younger generation, the atheists, the panslavs, the Russian fanatical sects, hermits and priests; falls incidentally under the influence of a Jesuit propagandist, a Pole, and descends to the very depths by joining the sect of the flagellants. At last, he comes to Christ and the Russian soil—the Russian Christ and the Russian God.

And while these images and scenes for his next book are swirling around Dostoevsky's mind putting him in a hyper-aroused state, he makes sure to include this parenthetical injunction:

> (For goodness sake, don't breathe a word of it to anyone: I shall write this novel of mine and I shall say everything to the last word, even if it is the last thing I do!)

This "to the last word" really struck me—the passion, the vision of Dostoevsky, yes indeed; but there is something else bubbling up in him that was taking over him at that time of his literary life, namely the prophetic! There was a message he had to write, that he had to get out of his heart to the Russian people. It is clear in the book that he was to write from this "and to the last word!" namely *The Devils* through which he foresaw the rise of atheism and nihilism in Russia, and how those philosophies from the west—Germany and France in particular—were in infiltrating the Russia of Christian Orthodoxy and the monarchy of the tsars. Dostoevsky continues in his letter:

> What I am writing now is a tendentious thing. I feel like saying everything as passionately as possible (Let the nihilists and the westerners scream that I am a reactionary!). To hell with them. I shall say everything to the last word!

To carry such a vision in his heart; a vision that he wants to shout from the rooftops—and, clearly, in his letters. A vision that he wants to squeeze out to the last drop on the page without care or bother about what anyone will think. And he wants to say everything "as passionately as possible." A day earlier, Dostoevsky wrote to his friend Strakhov …

> I am relying a great deal on what I am writing for the Russian Messenger now, but from the tendentious rather than the artistic point of view. I am anxious to express certain ideas, even if it ruins my novel ... for I am entirely carried away by the things that have accumulated in my heart and mind. Let it turn out to be only a pamphlet, but I shall say everything to the last word!

What pace, drive, energy of writing—just in a letter to a friend! You can feel that what he wants to say is ready to burst forth! He has been writing for the *Russian Messenger* as a journalist about current affairs from a "tendentious" or biased point of view, not, he says, from an artistic one. The artistic is the tendentious elevated to the transcendent. Dostoevsky has been researching and writing, which has conceived in his heart a work of art that must be birthed. And what will be birthed? Truth. A daring, audacious, prophetic truth. Truth that cannot be presented in any other way but as a testament from the artist's heart—right down to the very last word. And "to hell" with anyone who criticizes or judges or disagrees with him or tries to get in his way whether by ridicule or persecution of any kind. And even if it should be a pamphlet, a novella of some kind, regardless—he will say everything to the last word.

The only other writer I can think of with such an explosive voice is Nietzsche.[1] Whenever I read Nietzsche I feel like putting on ear muffs to drown out all the yelling. Nietzsche and Dostoevsky have pulse. They are combative. They grip you by the shoulder and drag you into their world, as if standing on the top of a hill somewhere, and demand that you look down upon what at first glance is a charming pastoral landscape but underneath it is more likened to a rotting corpse. They are both responding to their world prophetically, albeit from two different sides of the spectrum: Nietzsche hoping the death will lead to man resurrected as God, and Dostoevsky hoping that Russian civilization will avoid destruction by returning to a new love for God, the Church, one's neighbour and all creation. What Dostoevsky was indeed seeing while preparing for the book in which he would "say everything" was the fall of Russia to anarchy and atheism, the two of which together would usher in an age of great terror and destruction. And that the only way for Russia to avoid destruction was for her to return to its true foundation: the Holy Russian Orthodox Church and the sovereignty of the tsars. Nietzsche thirsted for destruction as a revitalization of man, while Dostoevsky wanted destruction avoided at all costs, and instead a return to Beauty, Goodness, and Truth.

As I sat in my seat on the airplane, a series of questions came to mind: While preparing the book in which Dostoevsky would say everything, was he able to see the fall of Russia to anarchy and atheism that would take place fifty years later? Was he able to see the brutal execution of the Romanovs under Lenin? Did he carry in his mind and heart the mass deaths under Stalin? Could he hear the cries of his countrymen from the gulags? Could he see churches up in flames in St. Petersburg? Is that the vision he carried that he sought so desperately to tell in its entirety?

Dostoevsky had jotted down notes in 1870, the ideas of which would fuse *The Atheist* with *The Devils*, whose chief character, however, was not to be an ordinary civil servant, but a wealthy prince:

"A most dissipated man and supercilious aristocrat," whose life was "storm and disorder" but who "in the end comes to Christ." He was to be a man with an idea which absorbs him completely though not so much intellectually as by becoming embodied in him and merging with his own nature always accompanied by suffering and unrest, and having fused with his nature, it demands to be instantly put into action. The prince is greatly influenced by a well-known religious writer who greatly in influenced Dostoevsky himself and who was to have figured in the novel. This writer's main idea Dostoevsky defined as "humility and self-possession, and that God and the Kingdom of Heaven are in us, and freedom too."

This is a powerful, yet subtle, idea for a novel particularly coming from an artist like Dostoevsky. To a North American mind, the solution seems shallow and trite as the prince has a 'come to Jesus moment'. But for those with an Orthodox mind, and Orthodox understanding of the Church and God and salvation, this turn of the prince—or re-turn—becomes a symbol for national repentance from atheism and anarchy to "humility and self-possession," and, as such, the Kingdom of Heaven itself. Dostoevsky with such a book wanted to impact his readers; he wanted to show the reader, indeed the world, the Way of Christ. Nihilism was eroding the spiritual identity of Russia. Rather than dance around the subject, Dostoevsky was planning to attack it. But in attacking the nihilism spreading through Russia he wasn't merely replacing one form with another, but rather pointing his readers, his countrymen, to the Way of salvation Himself, to union with God, His Church, and all of creation.

The theme of the great novel in which Dostoevsky would say everything to the last word was shelved for a more "tendentious" one. Indeed Dostoevsky was no stranger to money problems—one of the lingering and painful themes in his writing—and needed to make some money by writing something less serious and quicker than what his great novel would demand. Dostoevsky told his friend Makov,

> What I am writing for the *Russian Messenger* now I shall finish in about three months, and then after a month's holiday, I shall sit down to my other novel. It is the same idea I wrote to you before. It will be my last novel.

Dostoevsky went on to construct the novel that eight years later would become *The Brothers Karamazov*. At one point it was called *The Great Sinner*. It was indeed Dostoevsky's final novel before his death, and arguably his very best.

Prophetic Writing

As Christians we are called to be kings, priests, and prophets. Dostoevsky shows us what it means to write prophetically. He wrote in response to the storm he saw brewing in his time that would break out into mass chaos, destruction, and death. I believe he foresaw the Bolshevik Revolution of 1917 clearly, for he was indeed no stranger to revolutionary groups, having been in one for which he was exiled and nearly executed. And it wouldn't surprise me if his powerful imagination yielded foresight into the gulags and the deaths of sixty million of his fellow Russians. Whatever Dostoevsky saw or didn't see, he had the vision, the guts, the passion to put it all down on paper and publish it.

If you're reading this and you're an artist, do you have this sense of purpose and vision and passion? Are you currently working on something in which you are saying everything to the last word? Are you seeing things in society, are there storms brewing on the horizon, that you see and feel you need to reveal to the world? Do you go about your day with the gnawing sense that if you were to die unexpectedly without having completed that work it would be most devastating to you?

In these times of brewing chaos and unpredictability, may the Lord grant us the courage and wisdom to follow the example of Dostoevsky and speak the truth from our hearts and let it radiate out through our work. Let us work tirelessly each day for the glory and honour of God, and may He bless the works of our hands!

3

FROM REGRET TO GRATITUDE

HENRI NOUWEN AND CREATING FROM THANKSGIVING

In this chapter, Henri Nouwen shows us how to be a light to others through the movement of regret to gratitude. When our resentment turns to gratitude we can be more open to others and to our creating.

What is man that you are mindful of him, and the son of man that You care for him? You made him a little lower than the angels and crowned him with glory and honour. Psalm 8:4-5

Books for the Heart

There are certain books that strike right to the heart. They are books that are typically slim and seemingly simple, yet the more you dig into them, the deeper they somehow become. Thomas Merton's books are like that, as are Father Anthony Bloom's and Father Lev Gillet's. Henri Nouwen's books are like that too, though he has a different resonance, a different tone, than those mentioned above. Nouwen's books seem to be for people like me: those who live in cities and are full of doubt and despair at the predicament of modern technological society. They are more, it seems, conversational. Nouwen's ideas came to him while he walked the streets of Toronto. His books therefore tend to bear a markedly urban point of view that I resonate with as one who has lived in downtown Toronto, and who dwells in the urban part of Calgary.

I think of Nouwen's book *Life of the Beloved*, written for a friend who was in a state of urban ennui, or *The Wounded Healer* that opens with a case conceptualization of what Nouwen aptly called 'the nuclear man': the average person living in the technological world with all its ironies and vicissitudes.

The Beloved Neurotic

One way to describe Nouwen is that he was very human. He was a broken man who became the wounded healer for many of those around him. He had struggles and moments of despair and depression throughout his life. What makes him wonderful to read is he often bares his soul, sharing painful moments of failure, embarrassment, and rejection to highlight his theological or psychological points. To read Nouwen is to see into his soul, to see his brokenness, to see his woundedness, and thus, according to Nouwen himself, see his belovedness by God.

One of my favourite stories of Nouwen is when he was walking with a long time friend of his and sharing his problems, as he was known to do. His friend suddenly stopped him and said, "Henri—from the sounds of things you're just as screwed up as I am!" "Worse!" Nouwen replied.

Another story I found painful to read was when Nouwen invited a friend to have dinner with him, but the friend said he had other plans. Nouwen that evening decided to attend a party, and there standing among a group of people was the friend who had rejected his invite to dinner earlier that day! Nouwen left the party upset and deeply morose.

Reading these stories, our hearts break for Nouwen, or we blush in embarrassment. Why would he live with his heart so far out on his sleeve? And yet, for Nouwen, such vulnerability was the way to authentic living and creating. Nouwen's strength was his weakness, and his weakness his strength: he was a broken person—and he let many around him know it—but he didn't let his brokenness prevent him from being the wounded healer to others. He allowed God to show him how precious he was in the midst of feeling unloved, resentful, upset, and depressed. And that love is what drove him to reach out to others, to be present for their suffering, and to share in their brokenness as a loving presence to them.

From Regret to Gratitude

Creativity is vulnerability. Vulnerability is an act of offering ourselves freely to the other, including our present and past. The past for many of us can be a place of shame, regret, and resentment. How can I offer myself in a creative work if my past remains a closet in which I'm hiding my shame and regret? Nouwen opens us to this important area of creative becoming in a movement he calls "from regret to gratitude".

> When I think about what it means to live and act in the name of Jesus, I realize that what I have to offer to others is not my own intelligence, skills, power, influence or connections but my own human brokenness, through which the love of God can manifest itself. Ministry is entering with our human brokenness into

> communion with others and speaking a word of hope. The great paradox of mysteries is that when we minister in our weakness, we receive from those to whom we go. The more in touch we are with our need for healing and salvation, the more open we are to receiving in gratitude what others have to offer us.[1]

How does entering into ministry with our brokenness tie into creative work and living? When we enter into this vulnerability with God and others, we begin to shed the façade, the skin as it were of our false selves. We enter into a place where we can stand before God and others in truth and meekness and humility. Shedding the façade reminds me of Thomas Merton's well-known metaphor of how we wrap ourselves with experiences like bandages to somehow prove we exist. But that kind of existence is a mere illusion, a lie we tell ourselves and present to others. The artist is one who pursues truth. And pursuing the truth requires us to become true with ourselves before God first. If we can't stand before God naked and broken and bankrupt, then we can't expect to come to the blank page or canvas or stage in a real open and vulnerable way.

Here's more from Nouwen on the movement from resentment to gratitude.

> Resentment blocks action; gratitude lets us move forward to new possibilities. Resentment makes us cling to negative feelings; gratitude allows us to let go. Resentment makes us prisoners of our passions; gratitude helps us to transcend our compulsions to follow our vocation. Resentment exhausts us by complicated jealousies and ambiguities, stirring up destructive desires for revenge. Gratitude takes our fatigue away and gives us new vitality and enthusiasm. Resentment entangles us in

> endless distractions, pulling us down to banal preoccupations. Gratitude anchors our deepest self beyond this world and allows us to be involved without losing ourselves.[2]

Resentment is the act of holding on to our past, coddling it, covering it up, and withholding it from God and others. When we are resentful about or past and present, we are ashamed. When we are ashamed we can't be open to ourselves, let alone others. By holding our shame we prevent people from truly knowing us. We keep everyone at arm's length. And we cannot truly love when we hold our shame so tightly. Resentment is bitterness and loneliness. It is the ego running amok through the garden of our hearts as a way of protecting ourselves from shame. And when we hold our resentment, we can't let God transfigure it to gratitude. But when we move into gratitude, our past becomes a way forward for others. When we allow the resentment of our past to be transfigured to gratitude we can help others through their own process of transfiguration. Suddenly my past becomes a light to someone struggling with the same issues I did. And thus the past that I coddled, gripped onto, and kept from those I love becomes a gift I can offer to someone else.

Creating from a Place of Gratitude

When I write from a place of gratitude, I can weave narratives together from my experiences of pain and brokenness without holding back or candy coating it. I then create a place for the reader to resonate with or see their own pain and brokenness in a different light. Through this movement to gratitude, I then see that regardless of where I am in my past, regardless of the brokenness and shame, Christ is calling me to healing and restoration for myself so that I can become a light to others.

> Through the spiritual practice of letting go of jealousy and bitterness and forgiving and affirming others, we can make rivals into friends, and competitors into companions on the way to true greatness. Servanthood might sound like a pious idea, but it really asks for the humble recognition that our life is not our own to be defended but a gift to be shared.[3]

Letting go of our past is a spiritual practice, a way of reconciling ourselves to God and to others, of turning, through grace, jealousy and bitterness into forgiveness and love. And when we can let go of the resentment and pain of our past, and affirm love and community, we are then in the right place to create, to turn pain into prose, and offer it to the world. The converse of this way of being is hell: isolation, resentment, bitterness, a brittleness of being, possession of others, covetousness, and anger. It is how the enemy divides and conquers. In the animal world, a predator separates the weak from the rest of the herd before taking it down. The enemy does the same with us —pulls us into self love that is really self-hatred and compulsion, and isolates us from community, then dominates us sucking the creative life out of us. And what can we possibly create from that state of non-being?

We create what we are. We create the same drivel and pain that everyone else does who is held in bondage to their pain. We create more despair for others to consume, and wonder why we can't create anything else.[3]

Reclaiming My Past

To reclaim our past we first must have the courage to look deeply into it; to see the ways we responded to circumstances and the people around us, or to see how those around us may have mistreated us and caused us deep pain and trauma. This is very difficult work, and takes a lot of time and often help and guidance from others like a priest or therapist. But in staring into the abyss of our past, there is opportunity to heal from it, and perhaps even see in it a special grace and offering of restoration.

> In spiritual formation you may think about your life as a strong rock wall, resisting anyone and anything that tries to change it. Resentment makes us blind to God's carving hand, but gratitude helps us recognize the process—that slowly but surely we are being formed into a beautiful work of art; that we are being prepared to be a person who can offer our own pains as a source of healing for others.[4]

When we open ourselves to God and to His Love, we enter a place where He is able to restore us to who we are to become: the work of art He wants to create in us. And then the process of creating becomes one of the ways God restores us to the work of art He has created us to become—in essence, our true selves. As Thomas Merton observed countless times in his journals and other books, that salvation is the process of me becoming through grace more and more my self. But this becoming arises from a process of opening ourselves fully to God and giving Him our past, and being malleable and flexible in His hands to be healed and restored, and then offered to the world for the inspiration and healing of others. In this movement out of resentment towards grace, we enter into gratitude, into thanksgiving, into eucharist. "Gratitude is not a simple emotion or an obvious attitude. It is a difficult discipline in which I constantly reclaim my whole past as the concrete way God has led me to this moment and is sending me into the future."[5]

This is the opening of gratitude out of the darkness and pain of our past; the movement from holding onto my past, from coddling it, hiding it, to letting go and letting God take it. But not letting go into a meaningless isolated void, but letting go to the One who knows me and loves me, and created me before the foundation of the world; who sees me, and sees Himself in me for I bear his Image. And this God sees the work He wants me to do in this particular place in history, right where I am with those who are around me, and all the circumstances that surround me. In this divine vision for my life, my whole past becomes the unique movement of the loving God, my Lord Jesus Christ's pursuit of me and His commissioning me to the mission I am to take up: to be sent out as priest, prophet, and king into the world. To be His light in the darkness. My past therefore becomes the means through which others can see their own past and present as held deeply and lovingly by God.

> [Gratitude] is hard precisely because it challenges me to face my painful moments—experiences of rejection and abandonment, feelings of loss and failure—and gradually to discover in them the pruning hands of God purifying my heart for deeper Love, stronger hope, and broader faith.[6]

How often have we been transformed, moved, validated, by someone who has overcome a similar past or addiction or trauma simply by their healing presence in our lives; simply by saying to us, "Yes. I have been there, and I see your pain. But here's how I came through it …"

Our past is not our own. It is not ours to cling to and coddle, and use to keep the world at arm's length. Our resentments, our regrets, are not ours to use as pills of bitterness we swallow in self-pity and despair. Our past, with all the failure and loss and pain, is a story of redemption waiting to be written. Like beautiful pottery formed out of a chaotic mass of clay through heat and pressure and then the nurturing hand that carefully molds and shapes it, so our lives can arise out of the chaos of our past and be molded by the loving hands of God. And like the beautiful pottery offered as a gift to another person, so our lives can be the same: gifts that extend from the loving hands of God to those who are broken and suffering and can't possibly see their way out of their pain, resentment, and the addictions used to fix themselves. Our story becomes the gift we offer back to God eucharistically, and through His Love we offer to others. It's how we can be used by God to enter deeper into His love, and enter deeper into the authenticity of who we are—that no matter where we came from, or where we are going, we have been created by God and called to be His sons and daughters. He wants to heal our pain, heal our resentments, heal our calloused heart, so He can use us to spread His light to the world.

St Paul encourages us in this movement to gratitude by showing us who we truly are in Christ. He does this repeatedly through his epistles, but this scripture in particular bears some attention:

> I pray that you may have the power to comprehend, with all the saints, what is the breadth and length and height and depth, and to know the love of Christ that surpasses knowledge, so that you may be filled with all the fullness of God.[7]

St Paul reveals to us what he sees; he wants us to see with his eyes, like a painter. He wants us to know, to comprehend, with the rest of the saints, the heavenly hosts, what is the ineffable Love Christ has for us. Why? So that we may be "filled with all the fullness of God."

All the fullness of God?

Yes, all the fullness of God. I don't know what that means, but God does. And that is His vision for us. That is how He sees us, and brought us forth from the foundation of the world. That is what He is calling us to: loving union with Him, our fellow human beings, and all creation. But we have to do the work of offering all of ourselves to Him in the first place: of letting go, being vulnerable before Him and others; of being truly real and human. This is the work of spiritual formation, or, to put it more traditionally, the work of salvation—the work of becoming God's work of art.

May the Lord show us His great Love, and may we respond by giving more of ourselves vulnerably to Him and to those around us.

4

CREATIVITY AND HUMILITY

ARVO PÄRT AND THE SUFFERING OF ART

In this chapter, Arvo Pärt shows us what it means to create art as a product of spiritual practice. That creativity and humility are interconnected.

How long, O you sons of men, will you turn my glory to shame? How long will you love worthlessness and seek falsehood? ... But know that the Lord has set apart for Himself him who is godly; the Lord will hear when I call to Him. Psalm 4:2-3

Thanking God for Failure

Failure is really hard. I know that it is important when creating, but I have a hard time accepting it. The failures of my past in my weakest moments can arise before me all at once, and all I can do is hang my head and relent to despair and regret. I know better than to do that, but it still happens. And all I can do in those moments is ask God to deliver me, and then try to give thanks for them. But what about thanksgiving for a failure you're in the very midst of? It's one thing to struggle to thank God for a failure in hindsight, but what about a failure in the moment of its nascence?

One of my favourite videos of composer Arvo Pärt is his honorary doctorate acceptance speech at St Vladimir Seminary. Pärt approaches the podium and begins . . .

> In the Puhtitsa Monastery, Estonia, "Have you thanked God for this failure already?"

Have you thanked God for this failure already? In this address Pärt is showing us an orientation to creating art that is distinct from the way we might conventionally think of it. One imagines the composer or writer or painter in the heat of the moment creating out of a state of unflagging ecstasy. Not that creating this way is inadequate, but Pärt shows us something different. He shows us a way of creating that is deeply connected to the way of the heart. Pärt continues …

> These unexpected words were said by a little girl, I remember exactly. It was July 25, 1976. I was sitting in the monastery's yard on a bench in the shadow of the bushes with a notebook. "What are you doing? What are you writing there?" asked the girl who was around ten years old. "I'm trying to write music, but it isn't turning out well," I said. And then the unexpected words from her:"Have you thanked God for this failure already?"

There is a palpable honesty in this interaction between the little girl and the composer—as if between a man and an angel sent at just that moment to inspire Pärt for the rest of his life. Pärt gives us no indication of whether she was an angel or saint, but only the profundity of the little girl's question and the great impact it had on his life even decades later.

The work of art comes from our soul, through our body, and extends out into the world. According to Pärt, it is thus important that the soul is in a process of purification, and thus that the person is in a process of purification before God and others.

> The most sensitive musical instrument is the human soul. The next is the human voice. One must purify the soul until it begins to sound. The composer is a musical instrument, and at the same time a performer of that instrument. The instrument has to be in order to produce sound. One must start with that, not with music. Through the music the composer can check if the instrument is tuned, and to what key it is tuned.

The artist, the writer, as an instrument reminds me of the prayer of St Francis, "Lord make me an instrument of Your Peace." It is not enough to create art if it does not come out of a deeper spiritual practice of healing and restoration of the Image of God in us. For as instruments, we create sound. If the instrument is damaged or left out in the snow bank, or beaten and broken down and not fixed, it will not produce good sound. Moreover, the instrument must be tuned to the right key Who is the Way, the Logos, Christ Himself. The right key presupposes that there is a right way; that there is a way things simply are. We do not live in a random universe. There is a divine order to the cosmos which is seen time and again in patterns of nature and human life. Being properly tuned means that our hearts, our bodies, our minds are *attuned* to the primordial harmony in which all things have been created and all things are, which is love. However, if we live in the wrong way, if our sound is out of tune, if our instrument is not kept in good order, if we make our life all about fulfilling our passions, all about our envy, if we give into all our temptations, then we cannot expect to have much good to express in our art. For the soul, that image of God within us that we are called to bear in all aspects of our life—including, and I would say especially, in art—becomes distorted and darkened. How do we bear the Image of God? Through surrender.

> God knits man in his mother's womb, slowly and wisely. Art should be born in a similar way. To be like a beggar when it comes to writing music: whatever, however, and whenever God wants.

God knits us in His Image. The Knitter is the Holy Trinity. There is the fatherly Grace, the divine Word—the inherent Logic, Order, Harmony—and there is the illumination of the Holy Spirit. Art should be born in the same way: with grace—as a gift—with logic and structure and order, and with the illumination of the Holy Spirit giving the work an insight into the human heart, into life itself that is fresh and alive and transformative. This kind of work requires prayer, not ambition or ego. Rather, as Pärt shows us, like a beggar: Lord, however and whenever and whatever You want to create in me.

In Pärt's vision of creating art, of composing music, the whole creative process as it were is stood on its head, namely that the focus is not on creating art itself, but orientating our attention, our focus, on God first, and allowing Him to create through us.

> We [thus] shouldn't grieve because we write little and poorly, but because we pray little and poorly, and lukewarmly, and live in the wrong way. The criterion must be: everywhere and only humility.

There are so many books written about creativity and the process of creating things, but Pärt shows us something other: an orientation to God, our neighbour, and all of creation. We must not concern ourselves with whether we're creating enough, whether we have enough time to create, or just the right circumstances to create. Rather we should be concerned primarily about our hearts, our souls, and how we are living in relationship with God and those around us.

Creating and Doing Heart Work

Are we truly being loving? Is our creative work furthering or hindering the Kingdom of God within us? Is our creating coming out of a place of humble union with God, or is it all about our egos? One way of doing an ego-check is if you are prevented for some reason from doing something and you react harshly rather than with meekness and flexibility. Creativity is a gift we offer back to God. In such a way, whatever it is that we are inspired to do becomes an occasion for worshipping God, for offering our lives to Him in humility and prayer—and that includes the diffculties, the failures, the times when the creative work we're doing seems to be a waste, or a kind of thorn in us, something that we consider quitting time and again. If you feel this way, you're not alone. Read these words from Pärt:

> Music is my friend. Ever-understanding, compassionate, forgiving. It is the comforter; the handkerchief for drying my tears of sadness, the source of my tears of joy,

> my liberation and flight. But also a painful thorn in my flesh and my soul; that which makes me sober, and teaches me humility.

Whatever we are doing at a high level of commitment, whether writing or composing, painting or consulting, it should drive us further to humility—not pride. Pride is the downfall of life, period. The same with envy. A great deal of struggle within creative work is envy, which is fuelled by an existential insufficiency embodied in the sense that we are not good enough. Pride and envy kill the soul because it is in that state of passion that we tacitly make all kinds of deals with the enemy. And how many throughout history in the arts have made tragic deals with the devil all out of pride and envy and the unslaked thirst for fame!

The reason we are able to create in the first place is because we have been created in the image and likeness of God. And that is why for our creative work to be authentic we must literally drink from the source of Life Himself. Creative work requires a eucharistic life, which is the opposite of pride and envy, because in the Eucharist Christ, God Himself, becomes our all in all. His Life becomes our life. Through His Body and Blood we stand before Him as we truly are. We catch a glimpse of the glory and majesty of God that overwhelms all of our weaknesses. It is in the Eucharist that we can truly be healed and purified over time. Our work then flows out of that beautiful union with God who is Beauty Himself. Thus, if the work is taking me though a process of humility, if the work is a thorn in my flesh, then I must use it as a way to get closer to God through which it becomes a beautiful gift.

Thus the paradox of art as friend and thorn for Arvo Pärt is something I deeply resonate with. There's something sad and beautiful and broken and glorious about creating in such a way. In such a way of being, the making of art expresses our gratefulness to God for all things, including standing in the midst of another failure.

5
THE DESPAIRING ARTIST
IT'S NOT COOL OR ARTSY OR NOBLE

The despairing artist is often painted in a romantic way, whether Kierkegaard or John Cheevers or Woody Allen. But you don't have to live that way.

He drew me up from the desolate pit, out of the miry bog, and set my feet upon a rock, making my steps secure. Psalm 40:2-3

The Artist in Despair

How many images of the despairing artist do we see, whether in movies or in biographies? The lives of artists, writers, poets full of ennui, acting out in public. The whole John Cheever thing … John Cheever's daughter Susan was resentful of the romanticism surrounding her father's drunken literary life. Below is a letter she wrote to the *New York Times* in response to a sensationalized op-ed on her father's literary life:

> I was amazed to read James Atlas's romantic evocation of the fun we used to have in the New York Literary

> World. As someone who was a child at those parties where literary greats stumbled around lecherously in an opaque cloud of cigarette smoke, I can testify that for those involved—certainly for many wives and most children—that scenery was anything but fun. A tragedy of the generation that comes before ours was that many of this country's wonderful writers were also alcoholics. Every drunk—whether or not he can write—leaves a trail of destruction, desolation, confusion, and sadness which goes on for generations. It's certainly true that my father's novels and stories are redolent with romantic images of the perfect martini and the ideal adultery, but those stories are fiction—images created by a man who never found either.[1]

Susan Cheevers painfully captures the illness of the despairing addicted writer—what's sadder is that as a child of one of the great American writers she had to live through it. In some sick way, the opaque cloud of smoke, perfect martini, and illicit affairs are characteristics of 'a writer' as much as intense exercise and strict diet are for the elite athlete. Wanting to become a writer and reading the *New York Review of Books* and *The New Yorker*, and all the modern Canadian and American writers, I too was caught up in the hysteria of mania—channel my inner Kierkegaard (Am I in the despair of wanting to be myself or not wanting to be myself? Aw forget it!). So existential. So Woody Allenesque. But it's just not okay to wallow in it, to grow despondent and slothful, and try to slake it all through drugs, alcohol, and reckless relationships. That's instead the devil's playground, and the killer of any artistic work.

Then there's the whole charade of mental illness and the artistic life in general, as if art requires you to find any excuse to 'free your mind' and imagination. But despair and addictions are neither cool nor artsy, rather they are symptoms of a sick wounded soul that lead to the death of the person. So why is it glamorized?

Art and Manic Depression

Betsy Lerner's excellent book about writing, entitled *The Forest From the Trees*, has a chapter devoted to the topic of the mentally ill writer. Lerner was the editor of many great American writers, and, as such, had experience working with artists who struggled with mental illness and addiction. She writes with intolerance about the drama of the manic writer, and the self-indulgence that would lead to late manuscripts, poor writing, and overall destructive behaviour. She makes a distinction between the work of an artist and the person him or herself. Sure, a writer struggling with mental illness and addiction may have luminous insights into the human condition, but you wouldn't necessarily want to live with them. And you might wait around to hear a book reading from a famous author, but after a while if they don't show up you're going to be let down. And as much as Van Gogh has been immortalized after his death, in his final months the people of Arles had petitioned that he should remain in confinement particularly after hacking off his own ear.

Come to think of it, Kierkegaard was quite manic too. Such a guarded man. He would write, then go to the theatre only to abscond after the curtain went up and the acting began. He'd rush home and write until intermission then show up again to drink and be seen regaling with many friends and acquaintances. Then just as quickly as he'd arrived, he'd dash off home again, and so forth. He collapsed at forty-two years old on the streets of Copenhagen, and died a month later in hospital. Some claim he died of tuberculosis; but there was a lot of madness in his life that was part of his orientation to writing. In reading Kierkegaard's letters, he would have been a very difficult person to be with as much as his writing so greatly impacted many famous writers, philosophers, and readers to this day. When you read Kierkegaard's journals— which by the way are quite marvellous—you get the sense that his despair comes from a rather bleak, Lutheran orientation to God and to faith, with that typical emphasis on doubt-ridden fear and trembling without the succour of the Beauty and fullness and astonishing Love of God.

Manic depression in the work of art can be a kind of attempted alchemy, a way of channeling something you think is unique inside in order for your genius to come out—a way of making gold out of something base. And it is base. But then you get to the bottom of all that acting out, all the self-aggrandizement that you used to wrap around yourself, and realize it is really nothing new and that you're just a regular person deceived into thinking your despair makes you truly artistic. Nevertheless, the world romanticizes self destructive writers because it likes to promote illness and brokenness—indeed it goes farther than that and celebrates it. And that influences the next generation of writers and artists who believe they have to go farther and deeper into madness to gain acceptance and some kind of artistic aura.

More on Mania

In Kay Redfield Jamison's book on manic depression, entitled *Touched by Fire*, she observes that many artists believe that extremes in emotional experiences and suffering are not only a normal part of human life, but also essential to creativity and artistic production. Such artists also believe that psychotherapeutic and even psychiatric help will necessarily quash the creative impulse thus rendering them lifeless bodies without the ability to create at all. Betsy Lerner's answer is that regardless of whether or not you could see William Blake on the analyst's couch or Hemingway musing to his therapist about his fetish for cats, if you can't get your work done because of outrageous self-destructive behaviour, or you are sacrificing loved ones at the altar of the god of art—which is really you—then you need to get help, and help is available. You can have both: a good stable life, and all the art you can possibly create.

And if the reality of your life of self-destruction isn't enough to give you pause, then think about, at a really base level, what Hemingway would have done with a few more decades—or if he had spent some time on inner healing? Maybe he would have written even better works, and many more, while perhaps not having damaged his wives and his children to the extent he did. Anyone who writes a work with such awe as *The Old Man and the Sea* is certainly not bereft of spiritual understanding and wisdom—not to mention his absolute love for marine biology, especially marlins.[2] For someone like Hemingway, would more years of writing and a good home life been worth some time spent focusing on psychotherapy or some form of healing?[3]

Orthodox Psychotherapy—Yes, it's a Thing

For Orthodox Christians there is spiritual practice; but that requires struggle, the sacraments of the Church, and a spiritual guide or father of confession. One of the best books on this topic is *Orthodox Psychotherapy*, written by Metropolitan of Nafpaktos Hierotheos. *Orthodox Psychotherapy* is an overview of the Church's understanding of what despair is, what its causes are, and the pathway to healing. Metropolitan

Hierotheos observes that psychological problems are actually issues of a darkened mind and an impure heart. Such a state of the mind and heart, he writes, is a result of a civilization built on the intellect. The intellect, or reason, has been established as the dominant faculty through which we live and work and make all our decisions. For Metropolitan Hierotheos, the dominance of the intellect in our civilization has marginalized the heart as the centre of the human being, thus perpetuating a civilization of the loss of the heart. There are many 'techniques' available today that are meant to cure the mind, but they centre on the intellectual thus perpetuating the problem. An intellectual process of healing ultimately fails because it focuses attention on the person as his or her own healer, which is a precursor for lifting up the self to the position of God. Such a heightened sense of self leads to egocentrism and arrogance.

Conversely, because we are embodied spirits created in the image and likeness of God, the return to the human heart is thus the beginning of the healing of the human being. If one discovers one's heart, when one's soul is purified and one's intelligence free of the burdens of thoughts, psychological problems are healed; but this can only be done by Christ through His Church and her sacramental life. In spite of seeming rigid and exclusive, this process of healing the human heart ought to be a source of joy and relief for the artist; for because it partakes of Beauty Himself, Jesus Christ, it is a truly aesthetic journey in which the creative faculties, as part of the overall soul of the person, are restored to their original harmony with the self and with God and, as such, all of creation.

The making of art is secondary to becoming like God. And becoming like God is a process of re-aligning our thoughts, actions, and desires towards purity. To become more and more like Christ, and thus enter a place of deep healing through His Love. Such a life is a movement towards greater simplicity, meekness, and humility. Modern technological life, conversely, is obsessed with thoughts, with thinking, with analysis, breaking things down to their component parts and analysing them—including the human being. Such obsession with thoughts leads to mental illness, particularly despair and meaninglessness. What Metropolitan Hierotheos lays out in *Orthodox Psychotherapy*, as he echoes the teachings of the Fathers of the Church, is an understanding of how the body and soul are impacted by one another, for good or evil.

Thus when I go through bouts of despair, I need to take inventory of my life: what am I watching? What am I reading, or not reading? Am I sleeping in through morning prayers or Divine Liturgy? Am I drinking too much wine over family dinners? Am I eating too much and fasting too little? Have I been consistently receiving the Eucharist? Is my focus on loving and serving others or primarily on meeting my own desires? But we cannot do this work alone. We need a father of confession or spiritual guide as well as the sacramental life of the Church to enter this movement of healing.

The Eucharist as a Place of Healing

The Eucharist is the place we encounter Christ, and He, by offering His Body and Blood, encounters us. The Canadian writer and iconographer Michael O'Brien places a premium on taking the Eucharist often, and there in those moments of standing at the throne of God offering Him one's work, as well was hopes, dreams, and despair. Here's St John of the Cross …

On that happy night
In secret I went forth, beheld by none,
And seeing naught;
Having no light nor guide
Excepting that which burned within my
Heart,
Which lit my way
More safely than the glare of noon-day
Sun
To where, expectant,
He waited for me who does know me well,
Where none appeared but He.

The encounter with the One "Who does know me well," and "where none appeared but He." Do we come to Liturgy with this sense of awareness of encountering Christ Himself, of receiving Him into ourselves? Or is it just something we do to appease God, as a formality, an obligation? (And God forbid we do it solely for artistic inspiration!) Or do we leave the house as if on a pilgrimage, and arrive at the church as poor hungry pilgrims seeking our true Home? Do we stand there lost in our own thoughts, or are we offering up to God as we are before His throne surrounded by St Mary, the choir of the saints, and the heavenly hosts of angels, our hopes, our dreams, our artistic work. Are we giving our brokenness to Christ as an offering?

St Mother Teresa understood her and her sisters' work as nothing without the Holy Eucharist which they received every day. In fact, St Mother Teresa would receive questions every day about where the sisters get so much joy and energy from. For to her, receiving the Eucharist is also about satisfying the hunger of Christ, for He is hungry to unite with us.

In the instances of Michael O'Brien and Mother Teresa and the Sisters of Mercy, the Eucharist is fundamental to their work, because in it, in the life of the Eucharist, we partake of Life Himself, the Divine Logos, the One Who Is, the Logic and Principle of all being, the One Who created heaven and earth, who spoke the Mind of the Father. And thus for all of us who have sought to become His, partaking of His divine Nature is foundational for our entire lives, and for all the work we do, whether artistic, or service, or whatever else. And artistically speaking, many seek inspiration through different means. For us Christians, receiving Christ in the Eucharist is the highest experience we can have as human beings—to become one with our Creator and, through Him, one with all creation.

Return to the Banquet Table

When I complain to my father of confession about despair and despondency, he encourages me to "return to the banquet." Returning to the banquet is the antithesis of despair; it is the proper and efficacious way through the despair—not by my own bootstraps, but by the One who waits for my return and does know me well. No one else can lead me through despair into Faith, Hope, and Love—only my Lord Jesus Christ. I love the imagery St John of the Cross paints, the evening through which the soul moves in secret. It is a movement between you and Christ, and yet it is filled with the entirety of the Church! Nevertheless, there are those who like to keep their eyes closed through the Divine Liturgy so as to further concentrate on this loving union with God. There are those I know who are prone to leaving the church immediately after the blessing of the water and benediction so as to keep their attention focused on God, and not to let out the heat from the fire of love burning in their hearts.

Prayer Dissipates the Ego

Despair can cut us down. But it can also put a microscope over our egos. Prayer dissipates the ego. When we sit or kneel or stand before the icons, it is like a laser to the soul. In those moments we can enter into thanksgiving. "Draw near to God, and He will draw near to you"(James 4:8). It is for us to begin. If we take a step towards the Lord, He takes ten towards us. He who saw the prodigal son while he was yet at a distance, and had compassion and ran and embraced him. Again, return to the banquet table. With despair we often think we're screwed—that we'll never come out of it. And sometimes we don't want to come out of it. Sometimes it just feels like the 'artsy' thing, the Woody Allenesque thing to do. But it's never good. The heart is darkened and we are immobilized. But look at what the prodigal son did: he returned to the banquet of his father's table. He returned to God.

Despair is not the prize of artists. It comes when we drop our guard, when we live away from God—out there doing our own thing. There is nothing more freeing than freedom; but there is also nothing more enslaving. God is everywhere present and filling all things. He doesn't leave us, but we wander from Him. Despair is a way the enemy afflicts us. But it can also become, when struggled through, a pathway to virtue.

In *The Orthodox Way*, Metropolitan Kallistos Ware points out that when the soul advances towards loving union with God, the greater its adversaries, especially during times of prayer. Our struggles at prayer and during the Divine Liturgy are there to pull us back into egoism and despair and death. Those struggles are a sign that our hearts are passionate for God. And our struggle is to the death, and our labour unceasing.

Indeed the closer we come to God, the greater joy fills our hearts. This is the teaching of scripture and the holy fathers and mothers of the Church. And that joy-filled heart is then in the right position to create art. For Gogol, art is the introduction of order and harmony in the soul. And the objective of the work of literary art is to transform the soul of the spectator into a state of love and forgiveness. How often have you read Dostoevsky only to have your soul transformed into a state of love and forgiveness!

But when we are in despair we are under the false belief that we are suffering alone, that we are alone. But standing in Divine Liturgy we sometimes come to realize that we are in fact not alone. One of the ways the ancients understood identity is by the community one is a part of, and the place one is from. For instance St Thomas Aquinas's last name is not Aquinas. He bore that name because he was from the town of Aquino. And in this way, the Eucharist is that identity, for we stand in liturgy as sons of God together with His Church. We stand before God as His beloved, along with all the heavenly hosts and all the principalities and all the authorities, and then receive His gracious movement of mystical union with us. In a cinematic way, it is like hobbits standing among the throngs of elves and wizards as the victory cries rattle and thunder around them. And that glory given to God around His throne is directly connected to the battles His saints engage in and win here on earth. And thus we are never ever alone.

For as St Silouan says, "Keep your mind in hell, and despair not." Then he goes on to say …

> Understand two thoughts and fear them. One says, "You are a saint," and the other, "You will never be saved."

> Both of these thoughts are from the enemy, and there is no truth in them. But think this way: I am a great sinner, but the Lord is merciful.

And poof! The dissipation of the ego, and thus despair—at least for the time being.

6

ART AND THE WAY OF SAINTHOOD

THOMAS MERTON AND THE GIFT OF BECOMING YOURSELF

For Thomas Merton, becoming a saint was synonymous with becoming himself. And becoming himself was synonymous with writing.

You fashioned me, and placed your hands on me.
Your knowledge has become too wondrous for me . . .
For You possess my heart O Lord; You took hold of me from my mother's womb. I will give thanks to You for I am fearfully and wondrously made. Psalm 139

Merton by the River

Henri Nouwen told a story about the time he and some friends met Thomas Merton at the Abbey of Our Lady Gethsemane in Kentucky. "Bring some beers," Merton told Nouwen, "and we'll hang out by the river." Nouwen, who seems unassuming, had a large following of people and was known for hanging out with celebrities and the wealthy. I'm not sure what he was expecting from this visit with Merton, but the latter seemed to catch him off guard.

Nouwen and his friends hung out with Merton by the river and talked. "Nothing special," Nouwen noted, "just a bunch of guys hanging out and talking. And there was nothing particularly special or extraordinary about Merton either at that time," he continued. "He was a regular guy. Didn't say anything overly spiritual or grand or wise. But," Nouwen explained, "it wasn't until about a year later that the time by the river really opened up to me, and that's when Merton had the greatest impact on my life. I read as many of his books as I could get my hands on. I taught a course on him, and wrote a book on him. He's been very influential in my life, even though the time I spent with him was as if with an ordinary person."

From all that I've read about Thomas Merton, he was an extraordinary person with a deep intellect and keen artistic sensibility. Not only did he write powerhouse books like *New Seeds of Contemplation* and his classic autobiography *Seven Story Mountain*, but he was also a painter, poet, and photographer. He corresponded with some of the great writers of his time such as Boris Pasternak, Henry Miller, and Jacques Maritain. And yet, Nouwen goes out to meet him and stands alongside an ordinary man casually having a few beers by the river.

A Tree is Nothing but What it is

For Merton, becoming oneself is the process of becoming who one truly is. When we are truly who we are, we give glory to God. For that is the authentic orientation to the world as created in the image of God. What is the case with us humans is also the case for the rest of creation:

"A tree gives glory to God by being a tree," Merton writes. "For in being what God means it to be it is obeying Him. It consents, so to speak, to His creative love."[1] If the tree were to try to be something else, something it was never intended to be, it would be less itself, and thus would give Him less glory. Thus nature gives glory to God by simply being nothing but what it is, and what it has been created to be. As such, all of creation, each particular thing, is created with a logos, a purpose, an identity. Each being's logos gives it a one-pointedness, for instance a tree cannot be anything else but a tree—it cannot give up its 'treeness' and become something else, become other than what it is. And in this being itself, it gives glory to God and thus, for Merton, is a kind of saint. "The lakes hidden among the hills are saints, and the sea too is a saint who praises God without interruption in her majestic dance. The great gashed, half-naked mountain is another of God's saints."[2]

Do you look at a mountainside and see a saint? How about a bird that lands on your back porch, or a cow you pass by along the highway? How about in the gaze of your dog or cat? But what about you and me? The distinction between me and a tree is that God created me with freedom to either become myself or not myself. A tree simply is—its vocation is simply to be itself, to dwell according to its logos. But for us humans, it is qualitatively different. Our vocation is not simply to be, but to align our will to God in the creation of our own identity, our own destiny.[3] As human beings made in the image and likeness of God, we are free beings, sons of God. Thus we are not created to be passive beings, but rather to participate in God's creative freedom in our lives and in the lives of others. In this way we are, as Merton puts it, fulfilling our calling to "share with God the work of creating the truth of our identity."[4]

Merton's observations about sharing with God this work of creating the truth of who we are challenges the existentialists' perspective of identity by Martin Heidegger, Jean-Paul Sartre and others, namely that my existence precedes my identity, or my essence. For the existentialists we are thrown into a random void, a meaningless world. And we come into this world as a blank slate whose identity, whose essence, must be created on our own. And thus everything you do in your life creates your essence, your identity, in this random universe without God. Maybe we would want to have God around, muses Sartre, to give us the manual. But we don't. We thus must rely on ourselves. Merton understands this is a delusion of grandeur—that we can somehow kill God and do everything on our own without creating utter hell for ourselves. No—our lives are not our own. We belong to God. God gives us freedom, and He also gives us an identity that is not ours to somehow manufacture. Our identity is His image and likeness. We thus become more ourselves by becoming more and more like Him in this creative dance of being. Hence this "truth of our identity" that Merton writes about is contrasted by what Sartre called 'bad faith', what Heidegger called 'inauthenticity' and 'das Man', what Kierkegaard called 'the despair of not wanting to be yourself' or 'the despair of wanting to be yourself', and E.E. Cummings called 'gangs'. That is, what makes us human is precisely this choice, of being able to choose or not choose to be oneself. This awareness of the existential models of identity by Sartre and others opens us to this absolutely stunning insight by Merton:

> To say I was born in sin is to say I came into the world with a false self. I was born in a mask. I came into existence under a sign of contradiction, being someone that I was never intended to be and therefore a denial of what I am supposed to be. And thus I came into existence and nonexistence at the same time because from the very start I was something I was not.[5]

Absurdity, the False Self, and Sin

Merton calls the false self what it is: sin. Sin is the way of deception, of falsity, of creating a false image of ourselves to set before others to be worshipped, admired, and idolized—all out of the brokenness of the world that surrounds us and that darkens our hearts. Merton takes the existential concepts of philosophy and exposes them to the truth of Christ and calls them what they are. He reveals the true reality of the existential concepts of inauthenticity, despair, and bad faith as the masks we wear to hide our weakness and vulnerability.

Merton was at one point heavy into Camus. Camus was a friend and contemporary of Sartre, and wrote wonderful works of existentialism. He was keen to the fallen world, but as one who was a self-proclaimed atheist. Thus Camus did not use concepts that would be familiar within Christian teaching. Nevertheless, his observations of the fallen world are indeed poignant, which is probably one of the things Merton loved so much about him. Camus called the fallen world "the absurd." And what is so absurd about our world is the masks all of us wear at one time or another—perhaps all the time. That nausea you feel at a party surrounded by the idle chatter of people you know but feel so estranged from and misunderstood by. That estrangement you feel at your workplace where collectivism has taken over and devoured any sense of individuality or self-expression—and you realize it has happened to you as well. The artwork you attempt to create only to realize you're just trying to appeal to market-driven forces or a particular trend or particular kind of sound or style of prose.

It's a fallen world of masks that we are born into, a world we learn to adapt to by creating masks for ourselves to enable us to succeed or simply 'fit in' to it. And behind those masks, another generation of masks, and behind those masks another generation, and so on. The fall of Adam and Eve was the result of wanting to be other than who they thought they were. The serpent told them they could become like God. They didn't understand who they had been created to become—like God; to bear His Image and Likeness, and thus divine beings. The foliage they sewed together to hide their nakedness was the first mask.

Merton's writing about masks in the context of sin and fallenness is so poignant that to read it is to shine a flashlight into your soul—it hits between the eyes, but takes time for the truth to fully unfurl in your heart. "Everyone of us is shadowed by an illusory person: a false self. This is the man that I want myself to be but who cannot exist because God does not know anything about him."[6] God doesn't know anything about this person because the person does not exist—it is an illusion, a chimera. And God is all about reality. It is an illusion because this 'self' is fabricated, as Merton says, to somehow exist outside of God's plan, outside of dependence on Him, which is impossible. You put on your Raybans, get in your car, open the sunroof, crank up the tunes, and drive as if you're an autonomous set of atoms that are in no way determined by or contingent upon anything else. Frank Sinatra's *World on a String* is blasting, the sun is shining, and you feel like you've got a handle on everything—life is good! Total vanity. Total illusion.

> All sin starts from the assumption that my false self, the self that exists only in my egocentric desires, is the fundamental reality of life to which everything in the else in the universe is ordered.[7]

So painful! How often do I feel this way—that I can somehow 'order' the world through my decisions, my transactions, my freedom. Merton says this is the beginning of sin, for doesn't sin always begin with the assumption that I am my own god? That I can do whatever I want? That nothing else exists in this world but objects to fulfill my desires with? Isn't this why we construct these false selves in the first place? To somehow mold ourselves into little gods for others to bow down to and worship? Isn't that the pinnacle of celebrity stardom? But we all know it's fake—and that's the problem. Then, Merton writes, our lives are spent getting the right experiences to clothe our little god, our little idol with: education, accolades, promotions, awards, exotic cars and vacations. And then we carefully fabricate little icons of ourselves, called 'pictures', and post them on social media for everyone to see and be driven mad with envy. (Is it not then surprising that every iteration of mobile devices is primarily about upgrading cameras to do more with images of ourselves?) Merton says this is how we try to make the illusion real. Our whole lives are spent that way, if we're not attentive; if we lack the courage to look at ourselves and become more and more real by becoming more human.

Here's the coup de grâce:

> And I wind experiences around myself and cover myself with pleasures and glory like bandages in order to make myself perceptible to myself and the world …[8]

We do all these things, all the running around of life, drinking it all up to its dregs to hide ourselves from who we truly are: creatures of God—*creatures*. Vulnerable, weak, frail, and born into a fallen broken world. This hiding ourselves from vulnerability, from this frailness and weakness, this human-ity, is the despair of not wanting to be ourselves that Kierkegaard wrote about. But here's the flip side of the coin: we wear masks, we wrap experiences around ourselves, because we don't know who we have been created to become, and who in Christ we truly are: sons of God, ever loved and held and blessed by Him, called to become members of the divine heavenly hosts—not by merit or success or accolades, not by any goodness that exists in and of ourselves apart from what God has embedded in our DNA through His Image, but by adoption into His Kingdom out of ineffable passionate Love, that brought Christ to the Cross to defeat sin and death and hell and consecrate the cosmos and raise us up with Him.

What is the false self, the mask, for you? What I have noticed is the false self could be the 'self' we believe is the most 'authentic' to who we are. The writer. The poet. The jazz or blues man. The engineer. The Stanford grad. The Harvard man. The entrepreneur. The Top 40 Under 40. The innovator. The yoga mom. The hockey dad. What can be painful is when we realize that those identities we carry based on what we're good at can be the biggest masks we wear, partly because they have been created out of the comments, praises, and accolades we have received from others, whether individual friends and colleagues, or institutions we have received credentials or awards from. And we can tell what our false self is when we react to people or situations that strike at or assert themselves against that mask.

Think about it . . . Zoom in and look at many of the lives of famous writers or artists or musicians or entrepreneurs —in most cases a great deal of hedonism, ego, and brokenness. Why? Because their lives were all about preserving the identity that made them famous in the first place. It's like Tennessee Williams and his little essay *The Catastrophe of Success*: he had grown too big, too successful, too famous, and even, he lamented, too fat for his suit! In the success of the *Glass Menagerie*, the play he wrote that drove him to exceeding fame, he had lost the edge, the grit, the determination—he had fallen into sin. He was missing the mark of who he was. *The Catastrophe of Success* is Williams's lamentation that the idol of himself had created a living hell, and that he had to make some very deliberate and intentional efforts to seek health.

Now zoom in to your own life: when did you get into the most trouble? When you were too big for those around you? When your ego was on autopilot? Like Peter Gabriel laments in his song *Big Time* about his bed being a mountain range for his big fat head.

Becoming Myself by Becoming a Saint

When Merton became a monk, he was concerned about the writer that was on his shoulder. In his journals he writes a lot about writing. That writer on his shoulder was the false self, the mask he desperately wanted to shed. For greater than the desire to become 'a writer', Thomas Merton wanted to become united to God so closely as to be filled with His Love, in essence to become a saint which he believed was his and everyone's true destiny. When Merton was at Gethsemane the abbot encouraged him to write his story, which became *The Seven Story Mountain*: it had hit over 20,000 pre-orders before it was published, and sold over 100,000 copies in its first six months, and eventually went on to sell over three million copies. *The Seven Story Mountain* opened the door to Merton corresponding with some of the heaviest poets and artists and intellectuals of his day but he knew that the purpose of his life was not to become a great writer, but rather to become a saint. In a journal entry long after the success of *The Seven Story Mountain*, Merton writes about his desire to be ordinary—back to the river, some guys, Henri Nouwen, and a six-pack of beers . . .

But how does one become a saint? Merton answers this question beautifully:

> For me to be a saint means to be myself. Therefore the problem of sanctity and salvation is in fact the problem of finding out who I am and of discovering my true self. The secret of my identity is hidden in the love and mercy of God. . . . Ultimately the only way I can be myself is to become identified with Him in Whom is hidden the reason and fulfillment of my existence.[9]

And here's the clincher:

> Therefore there is only one problem on which all my existence, my peace and my happiness depend: to discover myself in discovering God. If I find Him I will find myself and if I find my true self I will find Him.[10]

Thus to become a saint is to become fully and authentically who you are: with all the gifts, and the challenges, and the set backs, the doubts, the despair, and seeing God working through all of it in a process of becoming more and more like Him, bearing His image and likeness—to become salt of the earth, and a light set atop a hill.

Christ tells us that He stands at the door and knocks. If we open the door, then He will come in and eat with us and we will eat with Him. That eucharistic image Christ presents to us in the Gospel is the process through which we become our true selves. We stand before Him as we are —broken, bankrupt, made of a multitude of masks—and

He offers His Love, His Grace, His Body and Blood to us for our healing, and to enter into loving union with us. We are His. We belong to Him. Any existence apart from His Love, from His Body and Blood, is an illusion.

We can thus sum up Merton's vision of becoming ourselves like this:

The purpose of our lives is to become our true selves. Our true selves are found by seeking God. When we seek God He opens us to a loving union with Him. When we are in loving union with God, we become our true selves, and therefore saints. That's the purpose. That's the focus. That's the direction, the movement of our lives—all of us.

Not to be writers or Stanford grads or Silicon Valley gurus. Not to be artists, or evangelists or preachers; not to be the teacher, the orator, or philharmonic conductor—but simply who we are. To become more and more like God, and therefore more and more who we've been created to become. And when we are living through that identity, all the other things will be added to us. But they will be directed in the right way, towards the right mark, and for the right purpose. We can't do it by ourselves, for as Merton writes, the only one who can teach us to find God is God Himself, alone.

7

ART AND TRUTH

KNOWING WHO I AM AND WHAT I AM CALLED TO DO

Creating art means affirming Truth—who I am and what I am called to do. It is a process of truly knowing what's real and what's fake.

Teach me Your way O Lord, that I may walk in Your Truth. Psalm 86:11

Art is Not Relative

People think that art is 'subjective'; that it's just about one's relative experiences shot up with some paint on a canvas or rattled off on a computer screen. But that's not what art is. In the book *What is Art?* Leo Tolstoy gives a poignant definition of what art is that I will paraphrase simply as the following: a dance between the artist and God. Art thus involves a process of wrestling, of creating, of iterating that is, in essence, an affirmation of Truth, for God is Truth.

J.R.R. Tolkien had a lovely and intriguing term for this dance: sub-creating with God. Art requires this dance with God simply because we are not self-created, and the 'stuff' of our art is not self-created. God created us, and everything that makes us up as humans, and the stuff of the natural world we use as material for our art. God is therefore presupposed not only in every work of art, but in every experience, and every form of matter we use to create.

But let's go deeper into this subcreating with God. Let's look at what art looks like through our understanding of Jesus Christ as what St John affirms in his gospel as the Logos, the Word. Christ is the Word spoken through God the Father at the creation of the world. Moreover, Logos has another deeper meaning, namely principle, order, the underlying Logic of all that is. Therefore, what St John means when he states the truth that Christ is the Logos, he is taking a term understood by the Greeks through the ancient Greek philosophers such as Heraclitus, and showing its fulfillment in the Being of Jesus Christ. Therefore everything presupposes Him. He is Being Himself, and therefore the necessary and sufficient condition for the possibility of life at all.

This is also where we get order and purpose from. The Logos of the Father set the world in order out of chaos—brought light to darkness, separated the firmament from the waters, established the laws of nature. And Created humans in His image and likeness. That means that we are beings who bring order to things, who create things, who seek purpose in what we are doing. It's not an accident. We didn't evolve into this through some process of natural selection. We are created this way.

Art is an ordering of matter for a particular purpose or objective that transcends the materials themselves. There is a higher order that the work of art points to. In sacred works of art, there is the power to lift our gaze to what is true and real; to ascertain and participate in a reality that lies beyond ourselves—the holy. Unity, wholeness, completion, order—all ways we create and mimic the Creator. And all ways we affirm what is true.

What is Truth?

There has been an answer to this question since the creation of mankind. We were created in and through and for Truth. When in the gospels Christ told the disciples that He was going to prepare a place for them, and that He would return to take them with Him, St Thomas replied, "Lord we don't know where you are going, so how can we know the way?" And Christ, the Word, the Logos, replied, "I am the Way, the Truth, the Life. No one comes to the Father except through Me." Christ is the Way, the Truth of all that is. It has been that way since the beginning, in spite of all the myriad attempts throughout the history of ideas and thought and religion to somehow state or prove or affirm otherwise. But more importantly, Truth, the Logos, the One Who Is, is not just a concept or a mere force or energy, but a Person.

> Truth for us is not a system of thought. Truth is not created. Truth is a person. Truth is not limited to our apprehension of it. Truth transcends us; we can never come to the full comprehension of Truth. The search for Truth is the search for the Person of Christ. Truth is the Mystery of the Person of Christ; and, because he is a person, the Mystery is inseparably linked with the event: the event of the encounter. Mystery and event are one. The Mystery for the Orthodox mind is precise and austere reality. It is Christ and it is to meet Christ.[1]

Thus as artists we ought to become seekers of Truth and lovers of Truth. But of course this isn't just for artists.

Look again at St Porphyrios's affirmation that Christians should live poetically, that is to acknowledge the beauty of creation.

What is Real and What is Fake

Among the many prayers we might use at any given time, one we can often say in our times of pursuing art and beauty, is O Lord show me what is real and what is fake; what is true and what is false. This leads us back to our false self. To ask God for wisdom in every situation, and believing that He will show us the way; that God will give us the wisdom needed to work through every struggle, every trial of our lives. St James uses a striking analogy in the first chapter of his epistle. That when we merely hear the word of God, but don't do it, it is like looking at our face in the mirror:

> For if anyone is a hearer of the word and not a doer, he is like a man who looks intently at his natural face in a mirror, and after looking at himself, goes away and immediately forgets what he looks like. But the one who looks into the perfect law, the law of liberty, and perseveres, being no hearer who forgets but a doer who acts, he will be blessed in his doing.[2]

Do you see the duality? Do you see what happens when we hold to our Christian faith, our relationship with God, with Christ, purely speculatively or conceptually? We become divided within ourselves and with God and the world, and that fracturing leads to darkness within ourselves and a blindness to what is real and true. And is that not what sin truly is, the sickness of being that clouds our every thought, perception, and action? We ultimately forget the image of ourselves as it truly is, namely the Image of God. But only God can bring together who we are, our being, with what we do. To try to do it all ourselves leads to greater problems.

Where we can go wrong in the creating and making of art, or simply life in general, is putting what we do before who we are. Henri Nouwen wrote about this in his book *Life of the Beloved*: that when we make our life about what we do, what we have, and what people say about us, then we are up and down like a yo-yo. But if we live our lives from the place of who we are, what we have been created for (namely to love and be in love with God our Creator, and to love everyone and all creation), then it doesn't matter what life brings us, whether we sell a lot of art or not, whether people call us brilliant artists or not, whether we make a lot of money with our art or not, we will be living from a place of belonging and authenticity.

Back to Basics

We create art out of an understanding of, or a struggle with, the truth of who we are and the One who created us. The Holy Bible, the traditions, doctrines, and teachings of the Holy Church, and the movements of the sacraments through the Holy Spirit illumine us to the truth of our being, to the truth of who we are. Nothing in the world reveals such a beautiful and inspiring and redemptive vision of man.

What are we created as?

Children of God.

What is the goal, the objective, the vocation of our lives?

Loving union with God and all creation.

Living in Truth who is Christ is for everyone—it's how we were made. It's what we are designed to become and to be, and to do. And for those seeking to create, affirming Truth is the only way to go. This is where someone like Solzhenitsyn can say that to live courageously and to create courageously is simply not to give in to the lie. One word of truth outweighs the world. When we are growing in our affirmation of the Truth, we cannot affirm lies. We cannot create shallow nonsense designed to simply appeal to the baser parts of the soul. The love of Truth, the pursuit of Truth, the affirmation of Truth in our works of art will align us to what is beautiful and good, because goodness and beauty simply are, for they are the nature of God who is the Being of all that is.

Sometimes not producing art is where we actually need to be. Sometimes God wants us to put writing or creating away for a while and live with a fuller awareness of life and those around us. The point of it is that we are not 'writers and artists' first. Both of these monikers can be seriously damaging. How many people pursue art to be called that one thing: artist. Some people go as far as to say that their 'calling' is to be an artist. But what happens when you're down on your luck, when you're blocked, when a work you've done totally bombs and no one cares to even look at it? Are you failing at your calling? Where's your identity now? Back to the ups and downs of failure and success, of living according to an illusion, an identity you're doing everything to curate and prevent from cracking. A false self will always let you down.

So …

Back to identity:

Child of God.

Back to calling:

To become like Christ, to become like God and therefore more and more myself.

Back to destiny:

Inheritor of the Kingdom of Heaven, and reign with our Lord and all the saints and martyrs and heavenly hosts.

All the rest is simply documentation . . .

Writing, painting, filming, photographing, telling, pointing to and offering up to God all that we see.

8

THE VOCATION OF ART

A RESPONSE TO MICHAEL O'BRIEN'S LETTER TO WRITERS AND ARTISTS

Canadian artist and writer Michael O'Brien's letter to fellow artists and writers is all about the creation of art and spiritual practice—in essence, to become saints.

When You said, "Seek My face," my heart said to You, "Your face, LORD, I will seek." Psalm 27:8

We Are God's Work of Art

Michael O'Brien is a Canadian writer and iconographer. His three volume series Father Elijah is a literary thriller about a priest commissioned by the Pope to convert to Catholicism a powerful leader prophesied to be the Antichrist. Where the book could be written as a sensationalistic Christian thriller, it reads much more like Dostoevsky. O'Brien's iconography is also striking—a melding of ancient and modern form that is unique to his own aesthetic sensibility. Along with O'Brien's fiction, there are a number of essays that he has written on Christian spiritual practice and the making of art. His *Letter to Fellow Artists and Writers*[1] is an excellent introduction to this way of understanding and practicing creativity. O'Brien writes,

> We are God's work of art, says St Paul. Growth in the vocation is usually a series of countless small steps of faith, usually blind steps, because what God wants to accomplish most in us is the increase of absolute trust in Him.

The work of art is thus secondary. The work of art comes out of our desire to serve God with everything—these small blind steps of faith, allowing Him to accomplish in us more than just a piece of writing. He is calling, as O'Brien continues, for us to be instruments in His hands, to be like children, little toddlers, "trusting God to the point of rashness in His merciful love."

The work of God in us is for us to grow in our total trust and abandonment in His love and mercy. This growth can be painful, however, because the work of the artist tends to be purely in and for the ego, for the self.

The objective of the artist—the inauthentic objective of the artist—is to make work worthy of the moniker 'artist', to be called an artist by others. And not just to be called an artist, but to be a successful artist—to be a recognized artist by producing work that is recognizable. But that's the Promethean orientation towards art: the will to steal fire from the gods and manipulate it or wield it for one's own glory—what is called idolatry. It is also the way of despair.

But God's plan is different. He's not after successes—even for his Kingdom, but for us to belong wholly to Him. The real goal of the artist is to become more fully human, more authentically oneself, which means to become a saint, which is to be like a child in the arms of God in true faith and trust. And this is precisely where God wants us because then we are safe, our minds and actions and hearts are one-pointed which will make the work we do one-pointed as well. Thus to become little children in the hands of God is the path of the artist.

O'Brien continues:

> [God] is the true Father. This means you must go step by step, hand in hand with Him, even when you can't feel His hand, asking for each day's graces needed for each of your works.

What happens when we realize that the true objective of art is not to produce successful art at all? What happens when we see our true vocation as becoming saints, to grow in total trust in God, to walk hand in hand with Him—even when we don't feel it? Will you feel that paralyzing insecurity when you can't produce what you think is popular to produce? Will you be envious when someone else is more successful than you? Will you get depressed and fall into despondency if no one reads your books or you get bad reviews, or, worse yet, are met with dull indifference? Indeed, if the objective of our creating, of our life, is to grow in loving union with God and not to become famous or loved by others then our deepest failures can become the means of our salvation; our failures then become important points in our journey to becoming saints.

> Allow Him to expand your heart. Allow Him to create with the material of your life. Allow Him to make you

> more than you think you are. This long process will contain some sufferings and numerous expected joys.

This way of being, this dwelling in the Truth of Being, of allowing ourselves to be shaped and inspired by God through a process of becoming more and more like Him is the way of creating art. Our lives then become the materials God creates through. Rather than conjuring up methods and ways that we can try to 'get a handle' on the world and manipulate it for our own desires, we rely fully on the One Who Is, on the One Who is Being Himself, the One Who called all things into existence, without Whom nothing would be made that is made. The suffering then becomes part of this process of becoming by drawing us closer to God who loves us with an infinite love, that same love that called us into existence, and calls us out of the fickleness of the crowd—that lonely desperate crowd—into the arms of Love.

> Offer every suffering for the restoration of the Church and for the fruitfulness of your work—fruitfulness in the sense of good for others' souls.

This goes back to how God can use our past, our sufferings for the healing and inspiration of others. When we enter into the loving arms of God, the suffering can be healed and reformed, re-created for God's glory and purpose. The suffering is also the way in which, or through which, we enter into the suffering of our Lord—how we become more like Him. Suffering that isn't allowed to drift into despondency and hopelessness, but rather offered back to God in thanksgiving is the way of becoming more like Christ, and thus more and more alive and human.

The work of art, in this long process of suffering and numerous unexpected joy, is this death—it is the death of the artist, of the ego, of the self, and the rebirth of the saint; a love that never dies, that never fails. And in this death of the artist, this death of the ego, there is perfect peace—the peace that comes with being known and loved by God, a loving union with others and all creation.

The purpose of life is thus not to become 'an artist', not to produce art, but to love God and neighbour with the redirected energy that was once directed towards our egos in self love. Working hard, putting our lives in the hands of God, praying continuously then become the process for creating art, far beyond being "clever" or seeking "worldly connections," but rather to give everything—our whole lives—"even to the point of complete failure."

Complete failure? Why would we want that? Isn't the purpose of producing art to become a brilliant success? That's the thing: success has nothing to do with it. And besides, what would success in the context of what we're talking about here even mean?

Rublev and the Bell

This abandonment and complete failure is depicted brilliantly in Andrei Tarksovsky's film of the Russian iconographer Andrei Rublev. The final part of the film is a vignette about a boy named Boriska whose father was a renowned bell master craftsman—one who knew the secret to making the most powerful bells. One day some representatives of the Grand Duke arrive at the man's house seeking to contract him to make a bell. The man's son comes out to greet them and tells them that his father has died from the plague. But rather than let the men leave to find another bell master, the boy convinces the men that his father had passed on the secrets of bell craftsmanship to him. At first the men were doubtful. But it only took a few moments of insistence to convince the men that he could take on the entire job and guarantee its success.

The boy was put in charge of his father's former group of workers, who he largely contradicts taking over the entire project. He determines the right place to work on the bell, he discovers the right kind of clay for the bell's material, he hires and fires people—he is the key to every aspect of that bell, slaving over it, sleeping in mud pits on the ground where he collapses from exhaustion, rushing here and there, calling out one to do this, another to do that, solving major challenges and, in all, throwing his entire body and soul at this formidable creative challenge. Rublev is shown several times in the background. He has taken a vow of silence and has given up painting after witnessing the brutal raid on the city of Vladimir at the hands of the Tatars. But he is now watching this boy with eagerness and suspicion.

Finally the day comes for the bell to be to be tested. The Grand Duke arrives along with his men. The villagers arrive too, as do the clergy. The boy tries to abscond from the scene, but is halted by the Grand Duke who threatens him with death if the bell does not work. Finally the bell resounds with the greatest gong! The whole village and all the workers caked on with mud, and all the clergy celebrate. But instead of celebrating too, the boy runs away and collapses in exhaustion in the mud and trembles with sobbing and total brokenness.

Rublev gets down in the mud with the boy and holds him like a father holds his son.

"Why are you crying," Rublev asks, breaking his vow of silence. The boy continues sobbing then replies,

"That old brute of mine, my father, never shared his secret —took it to its grave . . ." He buries his head into Rublev while the latter looks off in the distance.

The entire time of creating the bell, of managing every aspect of its construction, of leading countless people towards its timely completion, of risking his very life for its sake, the boy had no idea what he was doing. Nevertheless, he threw his entire being into it; his entire being and all his faith.

Rublev still holding the sobbing trembling boy replies, "Let's work together . . . you'll be casting bells and I'll be painting icons. Let's go to the Trinity . . ."

In this beautiful and compelling scene of Tarkovsky's *Rublev*, the viewer is shaken by the naïve and formidable faith of the boy. Unflinchingly and with little doubt, the boy casts his entire body and soul into the creation of the bell caring for little else save the successful resounding 'gong' upon first being struck. This scene is an example of creative zeal—the faith required to create by casting yourself into the arms of God. To have the zeal of that boy—the courage, fortitude, the blind passion! And yet that is what the Lord in His love holds out to us. Michael O'Brien adds the following point of transparency:

> During the most difficult periods of my life God taught me to trust that He was and is doing something through me and in me—even when it seemed hopeless and radically insecure (which was most of the time). In fact these are the times when He can bring about the best growth in us, if we continually renew our willingness to understand this discipleship of trust.

And here is where creative endeavours become ascesis—for how else do we learn that trust but through the hard labour of our souls during difficulties, trials, painful moments—when things seem 'hopeless' and radically insecure? We undergo the discipline of trust through choosing it every moment. O'Brien continues . . .

> So in all of this, my advice for your work and your soul is that you ask for the grace to be perfectly docile to the Holy Spirit, and ask continually for everything you need, both spiritually and materially. Then the doors will open. Not by our will, but His.

It's so easy to rely on ourselves—to believe we can think our way through the difficulties of life, to become 'savvy', cover all the angles all the way to success. But that's not the journey. The journey is to become a saint, to become a simple flower that is orientated to the Light from which it receives what it needs for life. To live a eucharistic life, as O'Brien explains . . .

> When I conceived the idea of my first published novel, *Father Elijah*, I went to our local parish church and consecrated the 'impossible, unpublishable' dream to the will of God. I prayed before the Blessed Sacrament every day during the eight months I wrote it. I asked daily for the Holy Spirit and for an angel of inspiration . . . Strange to say the book was the easiest thing I ever wrote. Usually writing is a hard labour for me.

This emphasis on the Eucharist really struck me when I first read this passage; for I read it before I was baptized into the Orthodox Church. I had never read this emphasis on the Holy Eucharist before in relation to creative work.

But the Eucharist, because it is the physical partaking of the Body and Blood of Christ, is the Gift of Life necessary for the renewal of one's mind and heart and to be given sight: purification, illumination, deification. Again, one's creative work is an epiphenomenon of the greater life of one in Christ; one of the offshoots of becoming more like Christ and therefore more like your true self.

Through the Eucharist, the authentic Body and Blood of Christ, we enter into loving union with God—His ways become our ways; His thoughts our thoughts. And the emphasis O'Brien places on the Eucharist shows that we are not merely dealing with creativity for its own sake, but rather with a spiritual practice of entering into Love Himself in an ever deeper and fuller way, and He entering into us in a deeper loving union. And it is here in this Eucharistic union that we come to know the love of God for us, and learn to trust Him fully with our lives and those around us. Through the Eucharist we enter into the communion of Love that is the Holy Trinity, which is why Rublev's Feast of the Holy Trinity is so poignant, moving, and deeply loved by many. The whole movement of the icon directs us to the bread and the chalice through which Christ mystically offers Himself to us in sacrifice. Through this loving union with God, our thoughts become His thoughts, our ways become His ways, which also plays out in our creative work.

> Go to the very source. Go to Christ and ask for all that you need. Ask for growth in skill, for the spirit of perseverance, for faith and courage and love. Ask for a spirit of discernment in order to find your way through the fog of our time. Ask for humility and faithfulness, and for the ability to incarnate truth in beautiful forms. Be a

> servant to the One who is the source of all Beauty. Be His beloved. Be very little, and trust in this absolutely.

It takes faith to believe you're loved enough and good enough to ask God to grant you growth in skill, for the spirit of perseverance, and for faith and courage and love. And yet only God can grant those things to us. It really takes knowing and believing you are loved, for otherwise you wouldn't be asking God for those things; you wouldn't feel worthy enough. Sometimes we feel unworthy not from a place of humility, but from a place of insecurity and doubt about our worthiness and belovedness; that somehow we're no good and therefore unworthy to be blessed by God through our art. And it takes courage to choose to be small in a society that admires and follows top dogs. But you don't have to 'sell yourself' like that. O'Brien encourages us to be small and humble, trusting God for everything by trusting in His Goodness. O'Brien continues:

> Avoid at all cost anything in your thoughts or impulses that tend in the direction of ambition even disguised as ambition 'for the sake of God's Kingdom', self-promotion, manipulation, climbing the ladder of success. "Success" in worldly terms may or may not be what God has in mind for your life, but He surely desires that we each be blessed with the only real success, which is to bear the fruit He desires us to bear. It is not your task to make it in worldly terms. It is your task to respond to grace and to make works of art that will enrich and bless the lives of others. He will do the rest according to His holy will.

When I was younger, back in 1991, I found a U2 t-shirt that I really loved. On the back of the shirt was the line from the song "The Fly" that was released on the *Achtung*

Baby album which at the time was one of my favourites. The line on the shirt was about ambition biting the nails of success. I resonated so deeply with that line, reading it literally but ignoring Bono's frequent use of irony, especially throughout that particular album. I thought that if I only would have enough ambition, then I would be successful and therefore happy—I didn't quite factor in the nail biting that comes along with ambition: the stress, the pressure. A friend of mine is a developer who makes deals in the hundreds of millions of dollars. He told me that the key to being successful at negotiating such large deals is handling the pressure—Bono is right. But ambition and docility to the Holy Spirit are not synonymous. And there's the ambition for God's sake. Is it about us or about Him? Are we trying to decrease so He may increase, or are we using Christianity as a device to prop up our egos, our self image? Does 'Christian' simply become another bandage we wrap around ourselves?

The real success is to bear the fruit He wants us to bear, which may not look successful at all, and which may or may not include becoming a renowned or even widely read writer or successful artist. Doing nothing before God can be greater than all the ambitious action in the world. We instead of seeking our ambition, our success, our name or myriad books or paintings or music albums, seek God Himself; seek to enter into loving union with Him and allow Him to create through us. He will do the rest for us according to His will and great love for us.

All this said, there is an enemy who wants to destroy us, especially those of us who pursue our calling to be light to the world. The enemy will attack us at our creative gifts through despondency and sloth and the 'success-failure' polarity that is no less than an illusion. Here's Michael O'Brien's admonishment:

> Do not bow before the spirit of this world, no matter how benevolently and reasonably it presents itself to you. Over the years I have watched so many gifted young people lost their gifts when they succumbed to the false success-failure scenario. Their intentions were good, but they did not understand the nature of this struggle.

And then O'Brien goes on to show the kind of work one can be inspired by over against the shallowness of modern culture: Dostoevsky, Bloy and Flannery O'Connor, Rachmaninoff and Gorecki and Bach, the films of Andrei Tarkovsky and Ermanno Olmi; the icons of Andrei Rublev —to which I would add the iconography of George Makary and Jorge Kordis—and the post-Renaissance painters like Rembrandt and Roualt. "Learn from them," O'Brien writes, "humbly, obediently, submissively (from *submisso*, meaning 'within the mission')."

But it's difficult to learn from the masters of writing and art and music and film—especially these days when our attention is fragmented by technology. Try to sit still long enough to work through the silent pages of *The Brothers Karamazov* or three hours of Tarkovski's *Rublev* without rabbit-holing your phone. And not just watch or read them but learn from them, study them, watching and reading, listening over and over. The stillness and openness demanded of us to learn from them might set us up for the second part: reconnecting with God, the heavenly hosts of angels, the choir of the saints. How? Through prayer and stillness—we must work at it. It's really hard, but when it becomes part of our daily lives, or hourly lives, it will become part of our creative lives too.

> [We] have a grave responsibility before God and mankind. The arts can give visible form to aspects of reality including our faith, that are invisible. If an artist is steadily growing in skill united to God's grace, then new visual 'words' can evolve truths in the human heart . . .

This is a powerful insight: all it takes is for us to "grow steadily" in skill united to God's grace, then new visual words can speak to the human heart. In essence, steadily becoming a saint by becoming who we are: small, humble, and vessels that the Holy Spirit can work through for the edification, inspiration, and salvation of others. Writing with a vision and desire for saintliness, for blessedness, compels us to write overtly Christian works that edify and "reveal the glory of creation and the immensity of the Good News of revelation," for,

> In a historical era that overwhelmingly denies the sacredness of life at every turn, that seeks to 'decapitate' creation . . . authentic art can point the way to a true restoration.

We use our art to reveal the Truth of our Lord Jesus Christ and His Good News of liberation from sin and death. We become one with Christ through His death and resurrection, and the grace of the Holy Eucharist He freely offers us through His immense Love. As we chant during the Bright fifty days after Pascha:

> Christ is risen from the dead,
> Trampling down death by death,
> And to those in the tombs Bestowing Life!

Submitting our lives and our art to God to give Him glory and to be light to all those around us. May the Lord grant us His grace and the courage to ever turn our gaze towards Him and seek Him and the blessing He proffers us through struggle and toil and zeal for His great Love and in pursuit of our salvation.

9
THE WAY, THE ART, OF LETTING GO
ART AS SURRENDER TO CHRIST

The Way of Christ, and the life of the Christian, is the true art of letting go. It is a life of surrender to Christ.

One thing I ask of the LORD, this only do I seek: that I may dwell in the house of the LORD all the days of my life, to gaze on the beauty of the LORD and to seek Him in His temple. Psalm 27:4

Not Enough Time

I was talking to a friend of mine. He and his wife are both writers, along with having busy professional lives and all the effort that goes into tending to the growth and development of children. We talked about how difficult parenting is, but then the subject quickly shifted to writing.

"There's just not enough time," he said. "I work, get home, and I'm with the family—which is great, but by the time the kids are in bed it's ten o'clock and I'm too exhausted to write.

And I ask myself, Do I just push it, or accept that I won't be writing that day?"

"I get it," I replied. "It was the same with me for many years. Now the children are older, but there were many days when I felt that same way."

"It's like," he continued, "it's like life is moving way too fast, and I can't get a handle on it, and there's just no time to pursue creative work. And I don't know what to do. Writing takes so much time—the thinking about it, the writing itself, editing, rewriting . . . I just don't know when I'll ever have the chance to do it again. Life is just so fast. And it's not just me—I know a lot of people who are in despair because they need more time to do creative work, and there simply isn't more time in the day."

In that conversation I didn't want to get into the details of what he was saying; I didn't want to press him about his daily routine and what he schedules time for. I'm obsessed at times about the daily routines of writers and artists. What strikes me about them is how they have maintained this same routine over decades: they get up at the same time, have their coffee at the same time, go for a walk at the same time, eat at the same time, work from this hour to that hour, take their walks or exercises, have leisure time in the same sequence of activities day after day, week after week, year after year. But I know that's not what my friend was talking about. He was going deeper—he's a writer with a great deal of depth and perspective rooted in his Christian faith.

"You know," I began—going back to the conversation between my friend and me—"I've been doing a lot of thinking about this very thing, about slowing down and entering deeper into art. And this slowing down is the same slowing down that we must find in the heart. For what I have read about and learned in my own life is that art comes from the heart; and it is when our hearts are cultivated with good things, with prayer and silence, good things come out of our writing."

"I absolutely agree," he replied. "But it's so hard to slow down the heart. It's hard not to go faster to keep up and to write faster and work faster and try to get something done hastily because the clock keeps ticking and I don't want my life to end before I've got certain things done."

The Art of Slow

This way of slowing down the heart—of silence, solitude, and prayer—is the life of the artist. As St Porphyrios writes in his book *Wounded by Love*, every Christian must be a poet, they must have a poetic heart.[1] The Christian must have a quietness of heart to see the world as it truly is, and then capture it on the page. The writer's work is his silence. And that silence involves quieting the heart—resisting the vices that creep in when we are struggling to do something beautiful: the voices of judgement, the envy of others, the despair of having no time. All of these vices are those attached to a fast-paced unreflective 'life style' of freneticism, resentment, competition, envy, and greed—another way of putting it is the pursuit of mammon, which is the pursuit of all the things that give us a feeling of power over the world, a way that we can somehow get a hold on the world and use it for our advancement and power.

The Christian life is antithetical to the pursuit of mammon. A Christian, for St Porphyrios, is one who takes "delight in all things that surround us." The Christian sees "all things around us [as] droplets of the love of God," both animate things and inanimate things like trees and rocks and stars and flowers. It takes an artistic or poetic heart to see the artistry of God, "the little loves through which we attain the great Love that is Christ." Thus we must grow in love to become true poets and artists, to become true Christians, to become saints, for "Christ does not wish insensitive souls in His company. A Christian, albeit only when he loves, is a poet and lives amid poetry. Poetic hearts embrace love and sense it deeply."[2]

It is this struggle over the poetic heart that the artist, indeed every Christian, falls under attack particularly despair, despondency, and the desire to somehow 'fit in' with the world. There is the temptation to make oneself 'relevant' to the market forces and preoccupations that shape and drive the 'mechanical world'. There is an attack on authenticity of the person created in the image of God. For the enemy knows that if artists become depressed and degraded, then less people will be able to partake of Beauty.

But sometimes the time we take to write or create is not the time to create at all; rather it is time we need to sit quietly with God, to slow down our ambitious impulses, to make (kairos) time, not mechanical (chronological) time, to simply do nothing. This in itself is difficult, because we even want to rush through quiet time to move on to what is 'practical' thus stealing silence's spiritual rewards; to hurry and rush even through our prayers, as if truly stealing re from heaven to illumine our pages!

Father Joseph Shryvers—Trappist monk and friend of Thomas Merton—in his book *The Gift of Oneself* writes about the soul who is too hasty for spiritual improvement, and thus tries to do it all her own way. "She despises to give herself to God, to abandon herself to His providence, but in her own way. . . . She seems to . . . wish to enable [God] to hasten the work of her sanctification."[3]

Conversely, the poetic soul will seek to "go to one's spiritual exercises with a disengaged heart, to avoid all hurry, all over-eagerness, as well as cowardice, laziness, and routine."[4] The movement Father Joseph Shryvers explains here is a movement of hurry towards ones ego, and the using of prayer as a kind of idol to get a handle on what we want to create for ourselves, rather than an act of abandonment to God. I confess to having approached payer many times in this way, as just another device like my fountain pen and computer, or, baser still, a cup of coffee to hype me up.

The True Art of Letting Go

The real movement, the authentic movement, is one that subordinates writing to prayer, and to a heart that trusts God for all things. And in this movement, the creating of art finds its proper place, its right time, and thus becomes an extension of silence and stillness by becoming prayer as well.There is a book about producing art entitled, *The Art of Letting Go*. But letting go to what or whom? Letting go of what? The Way of Christ, and the life of the Christian, is the true Art of letting go. It is a life of surrendering everything to Christ. It's hard to get over the cliché of this term that everyone who has grown up in church has heard —like the country song, *Jesus Take the Wheel.* But if you really think about it, this art of letting go, it's immensely difficult and completely counter-cultural.

Our society favours almost exclusively what Ralph Waldo Emerson called "the life of the mind." We favour rationality, calculation, cost benefit analysis. We think about our careers, we stew over the smallest decisions, we break every decision down to its microscopic level through layers upon layers of 'analysis' terrified of making 'the wrong move', and we are filled with pride with the 'good moves' we've made. But that's not the art of letting go, rather it is the modern art of gripping hold of technique, of analytical process, to get us ahead in some fashion. In such a framework, trials and challenges are to be avoided at all costs, and we are no less than captains of our own ship and the gods of our destiny. That is not the life of surrendering all to God. For as St James writes,

> My brethren, count it all joy when you fall into various trials, knowing that the testing of your faith produces patience. But let patience have its perfect work, that you may be perfect and complete, lacking nothing. If any of you lacks wisdom, let him ask God who gives to all liberally and without reproach, and it will be given him.

Our trials as people and as artists and writers can make us stronger, can build patience when we surrender ourselves to God and lack nothing. And whatever we lack—wisdom, insight, strength, courage—we can ask God who "gives liberally and without reproach." He is our Creator, and we are His children; and He loves us and gives liberally to us. Thus,

> No spiritual exercise [—writing and art making included—] is profitable to the soul if it is made without the guidance of God. The soul's constant care ought to be to surrender herself entirely to God, then to take, one by one, the means which God gives her, under the respective forms He gives them, with the circumstances with which He surrounds them, and during the time He allots to them.[5]

The Way of the artist, of the poet, of the human being, this Way of letting go, is the true Way, for it is Christ Himself who condescended to become man, and surrendered Himself even to death for the life of the world. And we too are called to become this Way. We are only able to take our readers, our audience as far as we have gone ourselves, as deeply as we have gone ourselves into the Beauty, all the "little loves" of God's creation, and into the heart of God Himself. Like Moses with the stone tablets, we are only able to write what we ourselves have witnessed, the process we ourselves have gone through. The Way through is not more action. The Way through is hiddenness with God through stillness, solitude, and prayer, not only for our art, but most importantly that we may become His light for the life of the world.

10

ART AS SILENCE AND PRAYER

ST. SOPHRONY'S LIFE OF PRAYER AND ART

St Sophrony came to Orthodoxy and iconography as an artist. And yet, throughout his life after great periods spent painting, he would retreat to long periods of prayer. This chapter looks briefly at the place of prayer in St Sophrony's creative life.

Blessed is the man who walks not in the counsel of the ungodly, nor stands in the path of sinners, nor sits in the seat of the scornful; but his delight is in the law of the Lord and in His law he meditates day and night.
Psalm 1:1-2

Disclaimer

Writing about a saint reminds me of the way the Jesus Prayer was first practiced by the desert monks before the divine gift of the prayer rope to St Antony: the monk would have a pile of pebbles that he would cast into a basket with each prayer. The pebbles are light but when they add up or pile up in the basket, the basket becomes heavy. In this same way, I find taking on a subject like St

Sophrony or any saint for that matter—I can only write a single pebble and toss it into the great basket of his life. St Sophrony, pray for me!

Seeking Perfection in the World of Art

There is a wonderful book about Elder Sophrony written by a nun named Sister Gabriela, entitled *Seeking Perfection in the World of Art: The Artistic Path of Father Sophrony.* Sister Gabriela is a member of the monastic community Father Sophrony founded called the Community of Saint John the Baptist in rural Essex, England. In the book, Sister Gabriela gives us a glimpse into Father Sophrony's artistic life. Here we see how the artistic path of Father Sophrony led him for extended periods of time away from art itself, and into the time horizon of pure prayer.

> The battle between art and prayer, that is between two forms of life which require the whole of man, continued within me in a very intense manner for a year and a half or two years. In the end, I was convinced that the means at my disposal in art would not give me what I was looking for. That is, even if I could intensely sense eternity through art, this awareness is not as deep as prayer. And I decided to give up art—which for me was a terribly high price to pay.[1]

Is this not the nightmare of the artist, namely to give up one's art? Is art so expendable? Is art not everything, and the becoming an artist the highest achievement of human life? Is not the end of art, for those who create, the end of life itself? And what person who possesses a gift for art and an artistic vision would give that up for something like prayer? We can pray anytime. Prayer is the most casual thing: before meals, when you tuck your kids into bed, on Sunday mornings . . . What Father Sophrony is talking about here is a prayer that is much deeper. A kind of prayer that leads one into interior stillness before God. A kind of prayer that, subsequent to it, if there were any art left to be done at all it would emerge as another form of prayer.

When Father Sophrony abandoned art, he attended a seminary in Paris; but prayer continued to pursue him which drove him to Mount Athos. Sister Gabriela describes that in this world set apart for prayer, a place of endless kairos, Father Sophrony did not have time to paint —"his new life encompassed him totally."

> The isolation [of Mount Athos], coupled with the profound stillness of nature all around, favours prayer of the deep heart and thought of the great calm of the Kingdom to come. The slow eastern rhythm of Athonite life—an absolute contrast to the stupefying beat of our contemporary mechanized existence—adds a precious ingredient of spiritual comfort to this chosen place, since it helps one forget the temporal and plunge into contemplation of eternal mysteries.[2]

All the creative energy Father Sophrony had earlier given to his art was now concentrated on prayer. Father Sophrony saw prayer as "infinite creation," and "far superior to any art or science." And prayer is the greatest source of inspiration— over against artistic inspiration—because inspiration for Father Sophrony is "the presence of the power of the Holy Spirit within us." Such inspiration thus belongs to "a different plane of being" from what the artist or philosopher knows or understands or experiences, though such disciplines too can be understood as a gift from God. However, outside of prayer—that deep interior stillness—art, philosophy, even science does not bring one closer to union with God Himself or even intellectual knowledge of Him.

Reading and contemplating Father Sophrony's words leads to many questions: What is the creative act? How does creativity lead one to God? What are its limits? How is art infused with God? Can writing a story be like writing an icon? Father Sophrony, Michael O'Brien, Arvo Pärt, John Tavener, J.R.R. Tolkien, C.S. Lewis, Dostoevsky, Solzhenitsyn, and on and on—Christians who sought God through the making of art. What is the nature of this pursuit? It's like the statement about art Arvo Pärt made in his commencement speech: that we shouldn't worry about writing poorly, but rather praying poorly and luke warmly . . . Thomas Merton, Tarkovsky, Rublev . . . so many artists and writers, yet Father Sophrony ditches art for prayer, and then, out of and through that kairos of prayer, continues at times to paint.

> While on Mount Athos, Father Sophrony lived the centuries old traditions of holy Orthodoxy, and observed frescos, icons, and ecclesiastical art. In Father Sophrony's life of prayer, his days spent in his cell on Mount Athos, he found he had a lot of spare time. So he gathered up all the necessary equipment and archived technical notes on iconography, and began to paint icons. He became one of the first to renew iconography in its traditional form on Mount Athos.[3]

And yet, just as painting seems to fire up again, Father Sophrony turns once more to prayer. Sister Gabriela writes that "for Father Sophrony, submerging himself in ever deeper prayer and knowledge of God was of far greater importance [than art], a fact he writes about in different places."[4]

The heart is the well into which we dip our buckets for water of inspiration. Are we thirsty? For what? If the heart is empty and dry, and we reach down into it for inspiration, for creating, what inspiration will we draw from? And what is the end or purpose of our prayer? To create art? To be 'productive'? Or is it what it's intended to be: to grow in loving union with God and to see everything through the eyes of love. How easy it would be to slip into an orientation to prayer as artists as a kind of transaction: I'll spend my thirty minutes in the morning so that God will give me ideas and inspiration for art. Father Sophrony's orientation to painting is an example for us, namely that his pursuit of art was indeed suffused with a courageous and authentic pursuit of God. This loving union with God is not only the pathway to creating authentic art, but it is also the pathway for becoming our true selves, which is the beginning of authentic art.

The question is: Am I willing to give up writing indefinitely for a time, a period of time, for prayer? For me, to be honest, maybe . . . The temptation is always to get good and busy, or cut things short to get to work at creating something. Another way of approaching this conflict is to see prayer and art as integrated, not as opposed to each other. In fact, as we see with Father Sophrony, creating is prayer, and prayer an act of creating, of offering up to God our lives and everything around us. "For prayer," according to Father Sophrony, "is infinite creation, far superior to any form of art or science."[5]

Nevertheless, in response to get good and busy, I like to ponder this quote from Thomas Merton:

> Be silent in the presence of God, and find your salvation.

11

WRITING FOR THE APOCALYPSE

FATHER SERAPHIM ROSE AND WINDOWS OF CREATIVE TIME

Father Seraphim Rose was a monk, priest, and powerful writer. He believed he had a small window of time to write before the apocalypse. Looking through that small window at what he saw drove him to write with a force and pace that was unstoppable. He wrote as if he were running out of time—or running through time.

In them He has set a tabernacle for the sun, which is like a bridegroom coming out of his chamber, and rejoices like a strong man to run its race.
Psalm 19:4-5

Have You Got the Time? …

There are different kinds of windows. There are windows of space such as those that open out into the outdoors, that gaze out onto a traffic-lined street or a tree stretching its trunks and branches to the sky. There are windows to Heaven, such as an icon of the Holy Theotokos illumined by a small candle, and her meekness gazes out at you from the candescent stillness. And there are windows of time. I believe it is Henri Bergson who made a distinction between duration and time: time is exterior to the self, duration is interior. So there are windows of duration in which we receive a kind of calling to do something, and there's a window of time in which we fulfill that calling in the world outside of us. I suppose that perfect timing would be when windows of time and duration open simultaneously; perhaps this would be a kind of 'kairos' time, the right time to do something, a time that stretches out of time itself.

There is another kind of time: eschatological time, i.e., a time that is not yet. A not yet time is suffused with infinite possibility. We cannot comprehend the details of that kind of time. How are we to know and understand time in this way? How are we to prepare for that kind of time, for not yet time?

In the parable of the ten virgins, there was a duration and time unfolding before them that revolved around one extraordinary event: the presencing of the Bridegroom. The awaiting of the Bridegroom represented the not yet time; the time of waiting for the event; the time that stretched out beyond their comprehension, their control, their ability to know. Duration perhaps in this parable was represented by the lamps, particularly the oil in the lamps that was fuelling the flame, that was holding the light from being extinguished. All the virgins could do in the face of the not yet time of the Bridegroom was to make sure they had enough oil to keep their lamps burning. Five of the virgins' lamps went out; five of the virgins' lamps stayed lit. Why didn't the virgins with the oil share with those whose oil had run out?

The oil seems to be something internal to the virgins. I heard one interpretation that the oil is like a kind of creativity or uniqueness that could not be passed on to anyone else. It was ones unique calling, one's unique duration of internal and external time, the time to do things, the time the Holy Spirit is prompting us in our spiritual lives and vocations; an interior waiting that therefore could not be given to anyone else. It reminds me of the story told by the Desert Father St Sarapion the Sindonite. He was on a pilgrimage to Rome where he was told of a well-known recluse, a woman who spent her days and night sitting in silence. The saint met the woman and asked her, "Why are you sitting here?" She replied, "I'm on a journey."[1]

How's your lamp burning? Got enough oil? Do you have enough energy to rise and enter into that moment when time and duration are united in kairos, at the time of the event? The thing with being in that state of duration is that you need to be ready to act when the window of time opens and the event stands before you; that moment when you are called and must heed to the calling.

Fr Seraphim and the Time to Write

One person who has helped me think of the windows of time and duration in this way is Father Seraphim Rose. Father Seraphim's sense of urgency about work was directed most of all to the publishing activity of the Brotherhood. His constant concern was to produce as much soul profiting material as possible with limited time and limited means. In one letter, Father Seraphim wrote "Above all, let us remember that these are the golden years for us to produce what we can in the Lord's harvest!" And in another letter he shared what he had seen through the window:

> The future, it is evident, is very dark. We ourselves do not know from one year to the next whether we will have another year of printing activity or not. We pray that God will give us at least a few more years, if only to print those patristic materials which will help us and others to survive in the days ahead.[2]

Father Seraphim's vocation as a writer was directly linked to his sense of duration, time, and event. He believed that the window of time was small and under threat of closing at any moment. His interior waiting for the end times as it were was spent in prayer, liturgy, fasting, and writing—and he wrote like one who was running out of time, or running through time.

According to Hieromonk Damascene, Father Seraphim's biographer, Father Seraphim did most of his writing in his wood hut on an old manual typewriter often by candle light.

> He would never [take] time to warm himself up to writing by taking a stroll, etc. Whenever he was given time he would go quickly to his cell and immediately begin to work. First he would write out a plan or outline by hand, and then he would type an article from that. He would write fast, looking up occasionally. And he would often cross himself when he wrote.[3]

What an urgency and focus on his vocation of writing! We can see in Hieromonk Damascene's account of Father Seraphim's process the candle light of the writing station mirroring the candle light of his heart; his internal response to the 'kronos' time of the world becomes, through duration, the kairos time—the right time to write and produce and distribute Truth. Father Damascene continues,

> In the spirit of monastic humility, Father Seraphim avoided signing his name to what he wrote. In one of his [unsigned] articles, he wrote that some of the necessities for success in a monastic path outside an already established monastery were: "a lack of publicity and a desire to be lost to the world," the absence of any desire to "be somebody or do such an important thing as open a monastery," and a deep humility.[4]

Hieromonk Damascene continues in this vein of hiddenness that Father Seraphim wrote an immense number of articles often not signing his name to them. "His name never appeared in print. In the words of Alexander Pope: Who builds a church to God, and not to fame, will never mark the marble with his name."

Writing in Kairos

Father Seraphim is a beautiful example of how we can respond to the times through our internal sense of duration. Indeed in a marathon sometimes the athlete has to speed up in order to slow back down. How much longer will the window be open for us? For Father Seraphim writing in the seventies and eighties, the window at that time was threatening to close—how much more today!

Back to the courtyard, the virgins, the lamps, the awaited Bridegroom. A day everyone will face.

You wait . . .

How do you wait?

Do you wait as a victim of kronos, of external time?

Are you just standing not noticing the state of your lamp, the state of oil therein?

Or, like Father Seraphim, an example of one who kept watch over how the oil in his lamp burned, are you matching duration with time; are you working, striving, producing, making each day count in expectation of Him?

The lamps burn out around you turning from
flame to black . . .
But you hold on to yours.
Through prayer and vigil you have plenty of
oil with you to endure the times.
You stand.
You wait . . .
For the gate to open,
And you meet Him face to face,
And the light of your lamp is eclipsed by the
radiant splendour
Of Infinite Love Himself.

12

ENTERING INTO BEAUTY

ART AND THE LITURGICAL LIFE

The Divine Liturgy is an encounter with God, and thus Beauty Himself. We encounter God to know who we are: worshiping beings of God. This chapter looks at the Divine Liturgy through the observations of Father Alexander Schmemann, and Archimandrite Amilianos.

Praise the LORD O my soul! Happy is he who has the God of Jacob for his help. Whose hope is in the LORD His God. Psalm 146:1,5

Entering Beauty

Sometimes we catch a glimpse of Beauty that overwhelms us. We get gobsmacked by it. Knees knock together and we can hardly breathe, overcome by something transcendent and a power that is ineffably greater than what we typically experience.

Divine Liturgy is an entrance into Beauty, for we enter into the Way, the Truth, the Life of our Lord Jesus Christ, and He enters into us through His Body and Blood.

Andrei Rublev's icon called The Feast of the Holy Trinity offers a glimpse into the transcendent Beauty we encounter in partaking of the Eucharist, for it is where we stand in the midst of the Holy Trinity receiving the divine nature in us. And there are countless stories of what people have experienced during Divine Liturgy—the witnessing of saints, angels. Some have been known to send away the deacons because they find themselves in the presence of the Holy Trinity and need to be alone. One person once captured a photo of the priest as he was raising the chalice, and in the photograph he was bathed, enveloped, in light —but the light wasn't reflecting off the chalice, rather it was emanating from the chalice itself.

Doorway to the Enchanted World

Sometimes our Lord opens the enchanted world just a little bit to us, just a glimpse, a blink of an eye, to reveal His glory. It happened to me—just a glimmer of Beauty of the enchanted world that is realer than that of mere materiality. It was during the Anaphora of the Liturgy of St Basil.

> Priest: O you, THE BEING, Master, Lord, God of Truth, being before the ages and reigning forever;
> Who dwells in the highest and looks upon the lowly;
> Who has created the heaven and the earth, the sea, and all that is therein;
> The Father of our Lord God and Saviour Jesus Christ, by Whom You have created all things, visible and invisible;
> Who is seated upon the throne of His glory; and who is worshipped by all the holy powers.
>
> Deacon: You who are seated stand!

> Priest: Before Whom stand the angels, the archangels, the principalities, the authorities, the thrones, the dominions, and the powers.
>
> Deacon: Look towards the east!
>
> Priest: You are He around Whom stand the cherubim full of eyes, and the seraphim with six wings, praising continuously without ceasing saying—
>
> Deacon: Let us attend!

And then comes the part that we the people sing—we are singing what we are seeing as we're standing before the throne of God surrounded by all the heavenly hosts!

> People: The cherubim worship You, and the seraphim glorify You, proclaiming and saying, Holy holy holy Lord of Hosts, Heaven and earth are full of Your holy glory!

In the Nexus of Heaven and Earth

And there I was, standing at the throne of God with all the authorities, all the principalities, the hosts of Heaven, the saints, the angels, glorifying and praising God—I was standing there with them! I felt like I was one of the hobbits before the great Council of the Ring, and my vision was all hazy, but it was in my heart, I was standing there in my heart and surrounded by such beauty and glory. Father Alexander Schmemann puts it this way in his essay *Theology and the Eucharist* . . .

> Our earthly food becomes the Body and Blood of Christ because it has been assumed, accepted, lifted up into the "age to come," where Christ is indeed the very life, the very food of all life and the Church is His Body, "the fullness of Him that filleth all in all"(Eph 1:23). It is there, finally, that we partake of the food of immortality, are made participants of the Messianic Banquet, of the New Pascha; it is from there, "having seen the true light, having received the heavenly Spirit," that we return into "this world" ("Let us depart in peace") as witnesses of the Kingdom which is "to come." Such is the sacrament of the Church, the "leitourgia" which eternally transforms the Church into what she is, makes her the Body of Christ and the Temple of the Holy Spirit.[1]

How am I able to enter the throne room of Heaven, to stand before the Lord with all the principalities and authorities? And what else can I do but feel so small and so lowly, and yet so loved by God that I am welcomed not only to stand before Him and be among His heavenly hosts but also to receive His Body and Blood which He so meekly and lovingly gives! I felt so small yet so lifted up, so held, so loved!

Archimandrite Amilianos:

> So what are we doing when we are celebrating the Liturgy? We are having a reception, a supper. We invite as our fellow-guests the saints of our Church; we invite our father who has fallen asleep; our grandfather, our great grandfather, our loved ones who have left us; we invite the angels. And Christ Himself comes and provides His body and blood. And this is what we mean when we say: "having commemorated all the saints, let us commit ourselves to one another, and all of our life to

> Christ our God. Having welcomed all the saints into our midst, having implored them, and made them our helpers, we now give ourselves to Christ.[2]

After the blessing of the holy water and the Benediction, I left the church—returning to "this world"—and got in my car. As I drove away in the silence of the morning streets I got thinking about the beautiful opening of heaven during the Anaphora . . . Then it hit me: one of the reasons why we attend Divine Liturgy is to know who we are and the Kingdom we belong to. To know and encounter the power and authority of the Kingdom we have inherited by the grace and love of the Creator of the cosmos. There's a military quality to it—an aura of warfare and all the glory that surrounds cosmic victory. It's so Tolkienesque. It is such a tangible participation of identity to stand before God and then receive this gracious act of mystical union. It's so real, so regal, so glorious. Again, I felt like a hobbit standing among the throngs of Elves and wizards as the victory cries rattled and thundered all around me! And that the glory given to God around His throne is directly connected to the battles His saints engage in and win here in the place we inhabit on earth.

Again, Archimandrite Amilianos:

> And we know that St Spyridon "had angels concelebrating with him," and indeed every priest concelebrates with the angels and the saints. And the people, because they know this, sing the angelic hymn: "Holy God, Holy Mighty, Holy Immortal." The angels in heaven sing: "Holy, Holy, Holy" (cf Isa 6:3), and we thus repeat their words. In this way, heaven and earth, angels and human beings, all of us together form one choir, one festival, one song.[3]

Priest, Prophet, King

Father Schmemann explains our identity in Christ this way:

> "Homo sapiens," "Homo faber" . . . yes, but first of all, "homo adorans." The first and basic definition of man is that he is the priest. He stands at the center of the world and unites it in his act of blessing God, of both receiving the world from God and offering it to God.[4]

And the realization opened another key to our identity, the part of ourselves that the enemy loves to distort and lie about and manipulate us to wallow in shame and self-pity and isolation that we try to fix and medicate with unending chemicals and pleasure and experiences: That we are never ever ever alone. And yet, we leave the church, and return home to our work places and our homes and the places we frequent; we fall into our passions, our routine sins, our bad habits. We grow sick, sometimes toxic. And this feeds into our lives and into our art. But that's why the Liturgy is so important as a practice, as something we partake of again and again for the rest of our lives.

> We shall go to Liturgy again, we shall seize hold of Christ again. He will divinize us again. And so with constant striving, with constant progress—the priest in front, ourselves behind—we shall reach the kingdom of heaven. Do we go to the Liturgy with this desire? If so, we have secured the kingdom of heaven.[5]

The more I attend Liturgy, the more I want to attend Liturgy. The more I see it as a requirement for living. And as one pursuing art as a way to draw closer to God, I cannot think of anything better to do than attend Liturgy when and as often as I can. I realize in the Liturgy that it is God who is All in All, and not a particular piece of writing or some other accomplishment. To be human, made in the Image and Likeness of God, means that I must partake of Him as often as I can to mystically become more and more like Him. And as a writer, an artist, that means bearing that Image on the page as well as on the street or in my home or my place of employment. And then partaking of Him again, entering his Kingdom again.

> We have seen the heavens open in the Liturgy. We have seen the good things of the kingdom of heaven. We have received our dowry, the Holy Spirit. We have learnt that he whom we seek can be ours to embrace, that our sinful souls can take hold of Christ, and pull him mystically and invisibly within ourselves. . . . And when we leave, let it be with souls rejoicing, and let us "entrust our souls, and deliver our life to him." Let us entrust our souls to Christ, whom we have seen, and let us dedicate our life to him, and "let us set our hearts ablaze with the fire of his love.[6]

There is so much that has been written on this topic and so much to write on it! But does it matter? No. What matters is living a liturgical life by going as often as I can —to partake of Christ and to offer myself more and more to Him, and to become more and more like Him.

13
CENTRING THE HEART
PRAYERS BEFORE SETTING FORTH ON ANY CREATIVE TASK

Before beginning any creative task, I am learning that it is best to centre my heart and attention—to know the true task and Whom I am doing it for. For my work to become prayer, I must turn to God in prayer before starting out on it.

May the favour of the Lord our God rest on us; establish the work of our hands for us—yes, establish the work of our hands. Psalm: 90:17

Live and Pray

One morning after Divine Liturgy, I went to the front to receive a piece of prosphora from the priest. He said something to me in Arabic. I looked at him curiously . . . He said it again, this time in English, "Live and pray." This simple maxim has stuck with me since. Live and pray. To that end, before I sit down to do anything, especially creative work, I need to remember to centre my heart and align myself, my will, my intention, my purpose, to God. I found a little prayer that I pray from time to time when I remember it. It's called, simply, A Prayer Before Any Task:

Lord Jesus Christ my God,
You have said, "Apart from Me You can do nothing."
In faith I embrace Your Words, Lord, and I entreat Your Goodness.
Help me to carry out the work I am about to begin,
And bring it to completion. To You I give glory
Father, Son, and Holy spirit,
Amen.

Pray Through Stress and Worry

The completion part is always hard for me. I'm a slow worker, and have a hard time keeping deadlines for myself. I also tend to worry or stress about the work I'm doing: whether I'm doing it 'right' or not, or doing a good job—this is pride. I saw a quote by St Paisios once. It said, "If you are stressed, it means your plans are moving way ahead of God's." Apart from God, I can do nothing. And apart from his Goodness and His Love, I cannot bring His will through writing to completion. The prayer continues thus,

My Lord and Saviour, You
Became man and laboured
With Your hands until the time of Your ministry.
Bless me as I begin this work.
Help me bring it to completion.
Lord enlighten my mind and
Strengthen my body, That I may accomplish my task
According to Your holy will.
Guide me to bring about works
Of goodness to your service and glory, Amen.

Through a prayer like this, I hope to be merely a little pencil in the hand of God, as Mother Teresa prayed. Or, to be a little flower in God's garden just doing what I can do with what He has given me. It's not my effort only—it's God and I working together. He brings my task to completion in His timing and for His glory. This prayer also gets my ego out of the way, and centres my heart on true Beauty, Goodness, and Truth Who is Christ.

For the real work of my life is the work of the heart, not the work of art—to know and to love God and all creation. Writing is thus placed lower and lower down the hierarchy. I have suffered when I have attempted to upend this chain of Being and place writing at the top—the writing being a moniker for ego and ambition. The real creative work is synergy: my efforts and struggles and God's grace and everlasting Love. The product is my self: I become the work of art that God wants to form and shape me into according to His Image and Likeness. I may be on the way to becoming a saint, but in no wise am close to arriving—what would that even look like? Saint Silouan says,

> The saints were people like all of us. Many of them came out of great sins, but by repentance they attained the Kingdom of Heaven. And everyone who comes there comes through repentance, which the merciful Lord has given us through His sufferings.

And again,

> Understanding two thoughts and fear them. One says, "You are a saint," the other, "You won't be saved." Both of them are thoughts from the enemy and there is no truth in them. But think this way: I am a great sinner,

> but the Lord is merciful. He loves people very much, and will forgive my sins.

To this end, more important than anything else I can do on this earth—even greater than writing 'the next great novel'— is to enter into loving union with God, and there find my true identity, my authentic self, and my deepest transformation into His living Image. Thomas Merton's Journals contain many such prayers: that he may become a saint, and that he may be ever filled with God's Love.

> This is my solitude, to be separated from myself so that I am able to love You alone, to love You so much that I no longer realize that I am loving anything. For such a realization implies a consciousness of a self that is separated from You. I no longer desire to be myself but to find myself transformed in You so that there is no 'myself' but onlyYourself. That is when I will be what you have willed to make me from all eternity: not myself but Love. This will be fulfilled in me, as You will it to be fulfilled. Your reason for the creation of the world, and men in it.[1]

So I sit down at my desk to write. But before I do, when I remember to do it, I make the sign of the cross in the name of the Father, of the Son, and of the Holy Spirit. I bow my head and close my eyes, and I ask God to forgive my sins, to purify my heart, and to create in and through me what He wishes to create—in His timing and according to His Love and Goodness. Then, under the icons of Christ and St Mary, and through the prayers of St Patrick, St Moses the Strong, and St Mary of Egypt, I begin—knowing that I am the work of art the Creator seeks to create through my creating. And when I get up, when I am done, when my timer is up and I turn off my lights and enter the rest of my day, I remember what my priest tells me now almost every time I meet him to receive a little piece of prosphora after liturgy: “Live and pray.”

14

REFLECTING UNCREATED LIGHT

WHAT C.S. LEWIS AND J.R.R. TOLKIEN UNDERSTOOD ABOUT CREATIVITY

C.S. Lewis and J.R.R. Tolkien were two exceptionally prolific and creative writers. They understood their creativity as a form of spiritual life, and as deeply connected to Christ the Logos. Their writing was a mission to lead others to Christ, and to impact the culture of their time.

Know that the Lord He is God: it is He that has made us, and not we ourselves; we are His people, and the sheep of His pasture. Psalm 100:3

Creativity as Entering into Beauty

Much of what is being written today about creativity is about process as a form of technique—a way of applying certain methods and formulas to reach a given end. What I am interested in and trying to capture in these jottings (or what Kierkegaard called 'crumbs' or fragments) is an investigation into creativity as a way of drawing closer to God and thus entering into Beauty, Goodness, and Truth Himself. In this desire for relationship through creating, the outcome flows out of a broader set of gifts I received at baptism, and given to use in various circumstances, such as being hospitable or charitable or speaking into someone's life when I don't even know I am or being, in the words of St Francis, "an instrument of God's peace".

The common books on creativity today are about how to become more creative or worse yet how to become an artist. Desiring to 'become an artist' or seeking to be called or admired as an artist is a particularly painful illness born of self-obsession. And putting artistic work under the banner of 'Christianity' can be particularly dangerous, for it attempts to sanctify the ego.

The movement of creating in relationship with God is seen, among others, in the Inklings. Aren't the Inklings, particularly C.S. Lewis and J.R.R. Tolkien, simply made up of people in a rather at times clumsy way being used by God to open the masses to the enchanted world? And would they be people we would call, as it were, saints? Tolkien was curmudgeonly and back-biting—especially about Lewis whom he was at times highly contemptuous of—and Lewis regaled in his love for beer and smokes.

One of my favourite stories is when Tolkien criticized Lewis for his insatiable predilection for beer. "Jack told me he was cutting beer for Lent," Tolkien scoffed, "which simply meant he was down to two pints a day!" Were they obsessed about becoming artists? Did Tolkien seek to be hailed as the greatest artist of his time?

No. They both simply wanted to use literature as a way to open people to Beauty, Goodness, and Truth. One story in Humphrey's book is about when Lewis came across some science fiction—a far cry from the classics of literature he was teaching in his classes at Oxford. But he saw science fiction as a way to reach more people than, say, Dante could. He told Tolkien that they needed to put their creative juices together and write some science fiction books. Thus there seems to be something missional about Tolkien's and Lewis's writing; something that took them beyond the mere sales of books and the fame they would accomplish through them.

Sub-creating with God

One of the main themes of Tolkien's writing is sub-creating with God. Tolkien's use of the prefix 'sub-' is highlighted by the definition in the *Oxford English Dictionary*, namely "Denoting inferior rank or importance, secondary or subordinate in nature." Sub-creation with God: this phrase was presented in a lecture Tolkien gave titled, "Fairy Stories". Included in that lecture is a poem Tolkien had written for Lewis, which was a kind of recording of the infamous talk he and Lewis had that brought the latter to a deep spiritual awakening that would change his life and shortly lead to conversion to Christ. In the lecture, Tolkien declared that in writing stories, man is not a creator but a *sub-creator* who may only hope to reflect something of the eternal light of God. Here's an excerpt:

> Man, Sub-creator, refracted light
> Through whom is splintered from a single
> white
> To many hues and endlessly combined
> In living shapes that move from mind to
> mind.
> Through all crannies of the world we filled
> With elves and goblins, though we dared
> to build
> Gods and their houses out of dark and
> light,

And sowed the seeds of dragons—'twas our
right
(Used or misused), that right was not
decayed:
We make still by the law in which we are
made.

We are sub-creators with God because we bear His Image, and are refractions of His Light, the Light being Christ Himself. Yet the light is splintered because each of us reflects that light only in part. Interesting that Tolkien wrote through the words of Gandalf in *The Lord of the Rings* that even Gollum bares a splinter of light. And no matter the worlds we create, we still create based on the laws placed in us by God, still bearing His Image and thus of "inferior rank or importance."

Thus to Tolkien and Lewis, writing stories reflects something of the eternal light of God. In his lecture *What is Christian Literature*, Lewis argues that writing Christian literature requires a level of excellence and an acknowledgement that all writing presupposes Christ, the Word. Thus in his own way, Lewis is echoing Tolkien's 'sub-creation' with God. Lewis writes,

> I admit freely that to believe in the Incarnation at all is to believe that every mode of human excellence is implicit in His historical human character . . . [Moreover,] applying this principle to literature . . . we should get as the basis of all critical theory the maxim that an author should never conceive himself as bringing into existence beauty or wisdom which did not exist before, but simply and solely as trying to embody in terms of his own art some reflection of eternal Beauty and Wisdom.[1]

Tolkien and Lewis had very similar understandings of what creative writing is and where it comes from: Christ, the Uncreated Light and Logos of God the Father in whose Image and Likeness we are created. Reading about Tolkien and Lewis has helped me understand that our skills and talents are not ours. In fact, when I consider all that goes into writing, even the breath I breathe while tapping the keyboard or drifting a pen along the page is given to me as a grace from God. And all that would simply not exist without the laws established by God before the creation of the world, apart from which there is nothing.

The Promethean

The converse of sub-creating with God is what Merton called the 'Promethean' understanding of creativity, namely that creativity is that which man has stolen from the gods and claimed as his own. Such an 'artist', according to Merton,

> [Finds himself] face to face with . . . the myth of the genius as hero and as high priest in a cult of art that tends to substitute itself for religion. This delusion is serious, and it is here that 'creativity' sometimes takes on a demonic quality which makes it one of the tragic temptations of our era . . . Here art stands out as the monument of genius, not as the symbol of transcendent spiritual reality but as the ikon of the artist himself. The artist becomes fascinated by his own gifts and by their supernatural quality. He renounces everything else, including morality and sanity, in order to devote himself exclusively to their magic. His life becomes the deliberate cultivation of experience intended to open up new depths in his genius.[2]

The alternative or converse of sub-creating with God is, in its fullest expression, the demonic attempt to create the world in my own image and likeness—a kind of magic that is wielded against the world that I ultimately despise and use for my own glorification. And thus I, the artist, am engaged in a movement from sub-creation in the Image and Likeness of God to a kind of sub-human activity in which beauty is not the object but rather the lustful representing of my own experiences. As Merton observes, if such experiences are "sinful, degraded, subhuman," this makes no difference. Rather,

> The genius with his magic soul has descended into hell for a season of satanically detached lucidity which frightens ordinary men. This assures him of his own superiority and confirms him in 'prophetic' vocation.[3]

Reading this, it is no wonder that in Tolkien's universe the orcs are simply degraded and demonized elves—the beauty they once beheld stripped from them as they fell into evil and the sliver of light extinguished. For us human beings, the image of God in us cannot be extinguished, but can be darkened. A human being can become demonified as much as it is possible for us, through God's grace, to become deified.

In his book on the Inklings, Humphrey Carpenter observes that the literary criticism of their time presupposed that "bad work" came out of "conformity and discipleship," and great work out of creative freedom, "a breaking forth from certain centres of explosive force" called men of genius.[4] But such a point of view, according to Lewis, was contrary to the New Testament in which "it is often implied that all 'creation' by men is at its best no more than the imitation of God, and in no sense original at all."[5] Thus "Lewis concluded that the duty of the Christian writer is not so much a desire for self-expression for its own sake, but in expressing the image of God."[6] From this we can arrive at the basis for all literary criticism the maxim, contrary to the misperception of the artistic genius, that an author should never conceive himself as bringing into existence beauty or wisdom which did not exist before but simply and solely as trying to in terms of his own art some reflection of eternal Beauty and Wisdom.[7]

Faith and Humility in the Act of Creating

For Lewis and Tolkien, as well as Merton, there is something desperately wrong with the artist attempting to create Beauty and Wisdom out of a process of self-expression and self-reliance, as if we are the Creator. No. The three of them are aligned that the only way true art can be made is when it is sub-created with God out of faith and humility, and out of an understanding that He is God and I am not—not just in art, but all aspects of my life. Writing, creating Beauty, means that I am engaged in the Beautiful, that I am encountering Beauty Himself—not as a way to somehow extract creativity through ritual (to get a handle on God and manipulate Him to write the next Pulitzer Prize winning novel), for that's the demonic orientation, the realm of magic. Rather I seek relationship with the One Who has made the entire created order, has protected, assisted, preserved, accepted me, had compassion on me, spared me, supported me, and brought me to the very hour—now—that I am writing these words.

St Porphyrios urges that to be a Christian is to have a poetic soul:

> For a person to be a Christian, he must have a poetic soul. He must become a poet. Christ does not wish insensitive souls in His company. A Christian, albeit only when he loves, is a poet and lives amid poetry. Poetic hearts embrace love and sense it deeply.[8]

This poetic soul comes from Christ, from His Love, His grace. What I glean from Tolkien and Lewis is that the way of creating is the Way of Christ Himself. Christ condescended to become man, so why should I seek to elevate myself? The way up is the way down—the way of humility, of understanding that the book I write is not a monument to myself, but should be a reflection of God's Love, and a reflection of my desire to unite myself more deeply with Him, for only He Himself is Beauty, Goodness, and Truth.

15
THE LIFE OF THE ARTIST
PAVEL FLORENSKY AND THE ICONOGRAPHER

What is the role of the artist in relation to art itself? Pavel Florensky inspires us through his account of iconographers and their spiritual life.

Bless the LORD all His works in all places of His dominion. Bless the LORD O my soul! Psalm 103:22

The Polymathic Priest

Pavel Florensky's book is entitled *Iconostasis*. It is a dense work about iconography and the iconographer—so dense that to attempt to synopsize it in a single chapter is laughable. Nevertheless, there's something important that can be drawn from Florensky's treatment of iconography and the life of the iconographer that can be inspiring for all types of artists—and for those who don't practice art at all.

Father Pavel Florensky was a philosopher, theologian, scientist, and art historian who became a priest in Russia in 1911. Though never a parish priest, Father Florensky found true joy and healing in serving the Eucharist. For Florensky, to carry out the definitive Christian Mystery of simple bread and wine consecrated into Christ's Holy Body and Blood was "the only true way of union and love." Father Florensky's friend Sergius Bulgakov, one of the great Orthodox theologians of the twentieth century, said of him that "The spiritual centre of his personality, that sun by which all his gifts were illumined, was his priesthood." On 17 August 1910, Father Flornsky was married. Between 1910 and 1922, he and his wife Anna Giatsintova had four children. Father Pavel was a well-known academic and lecturer.

When the Bolsheviks took over Russia in 1917, they made Father Florensky an offer: either go into permanent exile, or do scientific work for the Soviet regime. Florensky was eager to do the work, especially given the way the soviets were seeking to integrate long-separated fields of knowledge. Father Florensky chose scientific work—but on his terms. What were Father Florensky's terms? Donald Sheehan, co-translator of *Iconostasis*, explains:

> Father Pavel looked every inch the priest. In exemplary defiance of powerful atheist masters, Father Pavel would stride into crowded lecture halls dressed in cassock, cross, and priest's cap. The scientific vigour of his lectures could not, for the authorities, eradicate the image they saw before them: for even the most rigid of atheists could not gainsay the iconic reality of his priesthood.[1]

And although he could not publish his scientific work, Father Pavel wrote theological works, the final one being his 1922 *Iconostasis*. In May 1932, Father Pavel was made the highest member of the scientific committees. But less than a year later, on 25 February 1933, he was arrested.

The circumstances of Father Pavel's arrest are convoluted. There was a professor named Gudulianov. Gudulianov was arrested five years prior to Father Pavel's arrest. Gudulianov was told that if he wrote a statement about supporting the Nazis, and in which he would implicate a number of people including Father Pavel, he and his family would escape imprisonment. If he refused, he and his family would suffer further punishment. Gudulianov chose to write the false statement. But he needed others to sign it, including Father Pavel.

Wounded by Love

Now Father Pavel did not succumb to the authorities at any time. He believed that signing false statements and colluding with the Soviets would harm the soul. But while arrested, Father Pavel was given a meeting alone with Gudulianov. Gudulianov pleaded with Father Pavel to sign the statement of repentance for colluding with the enemy or Gudulianov and his family would be killed. But what about Father Pavel's wife and four children? What would happen to them if Father Pavel were given the death penalty? Such circumstances threw Fr Pavel into a grave spiritual crisis. Donald Sheehan continues,

> [Father Pavel] would well have known that to participate in the lies of state violence robs the soul of every shred of spiritual integrity, and that once truly begun, the destruction of integrity is nearly impossible to halt. Yet he would also know that spiritual integrity in Christ has unfathomable depths, for in that bare OGPU room in late February 1933, Father Pavel could not have helped but discern in the faces of the Soviet authorities the very faces of the Jerusalem rulers who had crucified Christ. And what is the Crucifixion apart from the willingness to accept in unconditional love the violence that is

> given? Moreover, Father Pavel would have seen before him the face of his false accuser begging him for life. And if Christ in crucified agony had prayed for his implacable murderers to be forgiven, what was he to do with this cringing accuser?[2]

On 26 June 1933, Father Pavel was sentenced to ten years in the gulags. While in the gulags, he continued his intense scientific work, but always as a priest by serving "the needs of the poorest, most ravaged prisoners."[3]

A crucial image survives the darkness—Fr Pavel saved the scraps of bread from his own meagre meals and fed them to the starving and dying. Everything had been stripped away from him—social meaning, dignity, freedom, family, psychological well-being, and physical health—except this irreducible core of priesthood in Christ: this is my body; take, eat.[4]

On 8 December 1937, Father Pavel was executed most likely by a single shot in the back of the head. His body was never recovered. Father Pavel was a living icon who in his suffering and persecution never ceased to enter into it bearing the Image of Christ the Logos Himself. By feeding his scant rations to prisoners, "there is nothing he can either do or say—he must now simply and only be; and in this simplicity of being he reveals who he truly is in Christ".[5]

Iconostasis

What does the iconographer do, according to Florensky? The iconographer opens to us to the reality of the saints who we "can hear coming out from [the icons], through the brush work, the self-revelation of the saints … not in words but in their holy countenances."[6] We witness the saints, "they have appeared within our contemplation" because the iconographer has "simply taken away the obstacles that hid their light from us," and have helped "strip away the scales that covered our spiritual sight."[7] And through the icon, by having opened us to the reality of the enchanted world, we gaze, for example, at the holy Theotokos and say, "This is She Herself, not Her image, but She Herself who, with [the help of the] iconographer, I am contemplating. As through a window I see the Mother of God Herself! And it is She Herself that I am now praying to face to face and not to an image!"[8] Now, the iconographer has not created the Mother of God—of course not. Rather, the iconographer has "parted the veil so that She, who was behind it, now stands as a real experience."[9] St Mary now appears to me, is found by me, and I am found by Her.

What does the iconographer do to create such windows into heaven from which the wood and the paint open one to behold the Mother of God? This is true Art, and thus authentic creativity. And indeed not just windows, but doorways.

Thus at the highest flourishing of their prayers, the ancient ascesis found that their icons were not simply windows through which they could behold the holy continuances depicted on them but were also doorways through which these countenances actually entered the empirical world. The saints came down from the icons to appear before those praying to them.[10]

For some, icons remained windows. For others, through asceticism and prayer the icons more resembled doorways through which the saint would appear to the one standing before it. But it is not only those who entered into ascesis that the saint appears as if through a doorway, but to others who may be the least likely to experience such an encounter. They encounter a "sharp penetration of a spiritual reality into the soul . . . that instantly shocks the viewer who is seeing, for the first time, one of the great works of sacred icon painting." But this "sharp penetration of a spiritual reality" is not merely subjective, but rather strikes the viewer in a way that is real, transformative, an encounter with another world just as real if not realer than our own. For "so indisputably objective is its impact upon the viewer, and impact equally physical and spiritual," that we can only describe such an encounter as "a beholding that ascends" to another realm.[11]

What Florensky is describing here sounds like the story of Father Lazarus El Antony of the Egyptian desert. His conversion from atheist to monk and priest began when he visited a church that held a renowned icon of St Mary. To 'observe' the icon, one had to prostrate oneself three times before it. Fr Lazarus had just lost his mother to cancer, and was deeply saddened by her death, a loss that at that time was a void no one else could fill. He describes that when he made the prostration, he heard a voice say to him, "I will be your mother." On the second prostration, he heard the voice repeating the same thing. He began to weep, he describes, as if for the first time in his life. When he made the third prostration, he heard the voice again, but this time he looked up only to see St Mary step out of the icon before him, her arms wide open to him and repeating the words, "I will be your mother." That was the turning point in his life. From that time forward, all he wanted to do was be with St Mary; and that desire led him into monasticism and ultimately to the solitude of the Egyptian desert.

But what is the life of the iconographer according to Fr Pavel? How does the iconographer create such art? And what I can't help but ask out of this study is how can I glean something from the iconographer to apply to art or creative work in general? Is there something within the practice of iconography I can be inspired by for, say, writing stories, or for just living a poetic life (according to St Porphyrios) that is to be the hallmark of the Christian?

The Consecrated Life of the Iconographer

Fr Pavel describes the experience, the occupation, of the iconographer as that of one "who sees that the world is sacred."[12] The authentic artist therefore is one who sees the world as sacred and filled by God. Such a way of seeing is the point of departure for art. But this art is not just a free-spirited act of autonomy and 'self-expression', but rather steeped in and guided by the canonical tradition of the Orthodox Church. To some such adherence to tradition would seem stultifying, a way of repressing the artist from truly and freely creating. But it is actually the converse. To the iconographer, the "truly creative, the presence of canonical tradition frees the artist's energy for new attainments, releasing it from the necessity of sterile repetition."

The canonical tradition in which they work is thus a gift of liberation.[13] Why is it a liberation? For Father Pavel, the artist is liberated from the prison of his or her mind, of his or her subconscious, the *logismoi* of transience, and is able to create, to represent, what is real. Thus such an artist is "throwing away the perfection of form and is, instead, taking hold subconsciously of the wrecked fragments of forms whose perfection—now accidental and imperfect—can only be wholly subconscious memory" that is falsely called 'creative'. Thus Fr Pavel distinguishes between true and relative art: that the authentic artist is not concerned about his own truth, "but rather the objectively beautiful and artistically incarnate truth of things—and he cares nothing at all about pride's mean-spirited question whether he is the first or the hundredth to speak this truth. If the work is true, then it establishes its own value."[14]

Modern art, as a form of modern thought, is a process of continuous deconstruction for the pursuit of 'originality'. Conversely, the iconographer is capturing things as they truly are thus opening the beholder to the potential for encountering the transcendent itself. The continuous process of dialectic in modern art—the constant craving for some new expression, some novel thing—is the result of the breakdown of any restraints or boundaries of artistic form. This breakdown of boundaries of form is the result of modern thought as freedom from boundary or restraint, whether conceptually or morally. This lack of formal restraints placed on modern art leads to its aesthetic undermining such that a urinal becomes a work of art by simply being placed upside down.

For philosophers like Nietzsche and Marx, the death of God is the opening of human freedom; but as we have seen historically, the unchecked freedom of man leads to mass hysteria and collective insanity. And this is certainly what Fr Pavel not only witnessed, but succumbed to: the brutal overturning of the Good, the True, and the Beautiful for the free relative fomenting energy of the masses. Conversely, it's the placing of limits on iconography that allows for a freedom of expression on the part of the artists in creating a piece of art that liturgically points one to God, His Holy Mother, and the choir of the saints. Hence the creative process leads the artist into "the objectively beautiful and incarnate truth of things," and therefore into the really real world, not as some kind of 'relative truth' that one discovers merely for oneself, but rather that same truth that is universal and for all.

But again, what about the freedom of the artist? Is the iconographer's freedom restrained, compromised by the canonical tradition in which he or she works? No, because iconography is living art wherein "the artist who bases his work on the canonical tradition . . . discovers in and through the canons the energy to create works wherein reality is the true object of their meditation, wholly certain in the knowledge that this work (if free) will never duplicate another's—though his actual concern is not with that issue but with the truthfulness shown in the work."[15]

Fr Pavel is saying here that the canonical tradition as a set of symbols, while seemingly restraining, actually is what opens the artist to reality itself that he or she stands before, worships, partakes of through the sacraments, and is ultimately filled with the power of the Holy Spirit. In such a way, and standing in such a place that is filled with the eternal God, the artist cannot create what is merely derivative, but only what is truly original and authentic. However, it is this standing before the eternal God as the point of departure for creating art that actually calls the artist and sets him or her apart from the world. A calling that requires the artist to live a particular kind of life set apart from the proclivities and preoccupations of the world. The life of the artist, of the iconographer, must be wholly offered to God, which is antithetical to egoism. They must therefore, according to Florensky, "practice a greater humility, purity, and piety, a profounder practice of fasting and prayer, and a more constant and deeper contact with their spiritual father." And therefore, iconographers, as traditionally understood, must "always put themselves under disciplines stricter than any given to them, becoming genuine ascetics in the exact sense of the word."[16]

Because the artist is conveying that which is beautiful and true; because he or she creates to invite others into a reality that transcends the disenchanted and 'material', there is a responsibility he or she has to live in greater humility, purity, and piety.[17]

What strikes me about Fr Pavel's insights into iconography and the life of the iconographer is the question of how this might apply to writing. Is Fr Pavel's vision of the iconographer solely for iconographers? Is not a life consecrated to God and set apart from the world for the writer too—indeed for all of us? Reflecting again on Michael O'Brien's letter to artists, there seems to be a responsibility for me as a writer as well to live more set apart from the world, and to pursue a life "higher than ordinary"—to become a genuine ascetic. What also strikes me about this vision of the artistic life of a Christian is that it represents the antithesis of the promethean way of creating art that Merton criticizes: rather than the artist seeking all kinds of 'experiences' as an elixir that one imbibes for creative power, the artist enters deeper into genuine spiritual life through the Church and her sacraments. That one becomes set apart through a life of repentance and sacrifice and loving union with God. Florensky cites the Hundred Chapters Council (Russia 1551) in which the precise conduct of clergy and iconographers was laid out. It concludes, "Let it be known, then, that the icon painter shall be meek, humble, and reverent, neither filled with vain talk nor empty laughter, not quarrelsome, not envious, not a drinker of spirits, not a thief or a murderer."

How would this apply to my life? Do I see myself as such an artist? Do I see a direct connection between my life before God and my life of writing? Florensky continues,

> [And] above all things, that he shall sustain in great mindfulness a pure chastity of soul and body, and that if he cannot sustain a pure chastity of the body he shall marry a wife by the lawful sacraments of matrimony; and that always and everywhere the icon painters shall attend constantly to their spiritual fathers, telling them everything always, and living always according to their teachings about fasting and prayer and all the ascetic disciplines, doing so with neither embarrassment nor willfulness, and always the true wisdom of humility.[18]

What would art become if we applied these same standards as the iconographer? What would writing become? What would film become? What would music become? What would painting, and architecture become? If art flowed out of the holiness of the artist, out of the goodness and saintliness of the person?

Indeed, what is laid out by Florensky applies to more than just iconographers. It applies to me, to all of us. And as such, the life of the iconographer expands out to the Christian life itself. Thus the artist returns to the fundamentals of Christian life and spiritual practice, not to become 'artists' per se, but rather to become saints. The purpose of life is to become saints, and let art flow out of the abundance of grace and mercy and love as one draws closer to union with God and all creation.

And with that, my reflections return to Fr Pavel himself and the gulags: the simple icon of a falsely accused man offering his meagre rations to the poorest and sickest prisoners on his way to death, and, thereby, radiant with the Image of God.

16

THE SPIRIT AND THE LETTER

ARTIFICIAL INTELLIGENCE AND AUTHENTIC WRITING

Technology provides ways for us to do things easier and more productively. Artificial Intelligence is becoming ever more a tool that heightens productivity. But can it create authentic art?

I lift up my eyes to the hills. From where does my help come? My help comes from the Lord, who made heaven and earth. Psalm 12:1

Underwood 310

It's 7:30 on a Saturday morning. I am writing this chapter, as I have been doing with all the chapters of this book, on an Underwood 310 typewriter. This typewriter was manufactured in Spain circa 1965, and it still, after some refurbishing, works very well. I suppose this makes me part of a group of writers who have sought after a more tactile writing experience—a kind of reprieve from the one dimensionality of the digital and blistering speed at which a draft can be sent from keyboard to screen to digital copy instantaneously uploaded to whatever medium and mass distributed to awaiting readers. In fact, this chapter began as a blog that emerged from some jottings on a paper journal in fountain pen and ink. So what I'm doing here in this chapter, and all previous and subsequent ones, is copying from my computer screen to my typewriter. And after some editing, I will re-write the whole thing on my computer to be uploaded to a publishing software on which the book manuscript will be formatted. From analogue to digital, back to analogue, and back to digital.

Why I'm sharing this process is because it seems to run counter to how creativity is emerging through various AI tools such as the GPT ('Generative Pre-Trained Transformer') technology. The first time I witnessed this technology my head was blown. Now, AI is doing so much from advanced research assistants to ghost writers to movie producers. And with the exponential growth of this technology, we are indeed moving into a different world that is changing even what 'creativity' means.

Like Hemingway—but Really Fast

But it was the writing in particular that initially dazzled me.

"This is sick—" I told Dan. "Like—what am I even looking at!"

"It is—and a bit scary," Dan replied.

Dan is my friend who is my go-to guy for everything technology related. He's been using GPT technology since it first came out, and is currently designing educational modules with embedded GPT processes so teachers can design learning engagements with the help of AI. Dan continued explaining to me the gist of what the technology could do.

"You can ask AI to write you a 'boy meets girl' bank heist thriller—in the style of Ernest Hemingway, and it will do it at lightening speed. You can then take segments of the story and prompt the AI to re-write it in various ways, and it will do it. You can take an existing story, like *The Count of Monte Cristo*, and prompt the AI to re-write the ending in ten different ways. You can break a story down into chapters, paragraphs, sentences, and it will do it. Look here: I've prompted the AI to write a Christmas story fusing *How the Grinch Stole Christmas* and *Batman*."

To my astonishment, the AI chugged away pumping out an entire story fusing two seemingly random things into a plausible piece of fiction—and it was pretty funny too. My head still blown, I continued to press Dan . . .

"Can you get the AI to make you a cover for the story—like in a book?"

"Easy—" Then, switching over to a program called DALL-E, Dan prompted the AI to design a book cover fusing Batman and the Grinch in a wildly Vincent Van Gogh aesthetic. Within seconds—seconds!—a cover appeared.

"Unbelievable!"

"Crazy eh!"

"You know," I continued, rubbing my face and eyes vigorously from the sheer astonishment, "this changes everything for writers and graphic artists."

"Well, it's going to further render journalists obsolete—especially those who write crap without writing anything original. Watch this . . . I'm going to prompt the AI to write ten tweets about the story . . ." And there on the screen in blistering speed appeared ten tweets about the story, one after another. "As you can see," Dan continued as the words of each tweet were sprinting across the page, "this is going to put a lot of people out of a job."

I couldn't believe what I was watching. It was the advent of a whole new world. I just gazed at the screen and those words soaring along at near lightening speed—I was speechless, dumbfounded, stupefied. Just when I thought I had seen it all, Dan broke the silence, again. "But there's another thing here that will blow your mind . . ." He prompted the AI to write code for the story so it could be published to a website. And right before our eyes, in perfect code, was the story.

It was all so unbelievable, so revolutionary—yes, so cool! But it was the prose that really struck me. How could AI pump out prose that fast, and to such precise specifications? Plug in a plot line, choose a style between Hemingway and Murakami, and whamo! Within seconds you can see the words cascading down your screen.

"Dan—the potential here is unlimited!" I exclaimed. "Books, movie scripts, articles . . . You can use AI as a ghost writer—I mean, what's the difference? Authors use ghost writers all the time. They lay out what they want to say, and how they want it said, and the ghost writer will put it all together. It's the same thing . . . Or, like collaborating with another author—"

"But with a massive genius brain!"

I sat back almost out of breath from excitement and just gazed up at the story of Batman and the Grinch all laid out in neat little sentences and paragraphs. My mind raced through all the potentials of books: non- fiction, biographical . . . How many could I write in a month? One per week? Five per week? The number was limitless . . . I left the office to run some errands but could not stop thinking about that GPT technology—so many possibilities, so much running through my head.

Art Means Inspiration

While running errands, I called my friend George—a true artist and writer—to see what he thought. To me it was a marvel of technology, this GPT. My mind was still spinning with myriad possibilities—books, movie scripts. We could publish 100 books in a year!

"George—" I said, speaking frantically into the phone, "this GPT technology is crazy!"

"Yeah . . ." he replied apathetically, "but I mean, I haven't used it before."

"It's a marvel!" I continued barreling over him with enthusiasm. "Think of all that we could be writing!"

"Right . . ." he continued with total indifference, "I guess it could be a marvel, depending of course on what you mean by writing, and what the purpose of writing actually is . . ."

As much as I respect George, he wasn't seeing it properly. How could he not be seeing it properly!

"But George listen . . . it's no different from working with another author or ghost writer. You can still write with it — you're just, you know, consulting a very powerful brain that's only getting smarter with each passing day."

George's silence betrayed his growing indifference. Finally, after more silence, he spoke up.

"Yeah, I'm aware of that. But look, the whole thing's so problematic. I knew someone once who used it to create a sermon on asceticism of all things. The AI delved into St Antony and the desert fathers. It distinguished clearly between the various types of asceticism, along with the spiritual advantages of asceticism. It even went into the Jesus Prayer. The sermon had all the right components, but came off totally wrong—there was something really off about it, like . . . where's all that content coming from, really . . ."

I knew I could get it straight from George. And for some reason I breathed a sigh of relief and returned to myself, to the present moment and out of the carousel that was my spinning head.

"I see your point—how is it in any way authentic . . ."

"Precisely . . . I mean, if the point of writing is to put words on paper, then by all means use a tool like that. But if writing is an activity that is inspired by God, then it is something that AI simply cannot do—"

"It takes a human being to receive inspiration from the Holy Spirit . . . it takes having one's heart open to God."

"Yes . . . And if I'm not inspired to write and thus need an AI then I have to look at what's going on in my life. I need to draw closer to God, not closer to technology. . . . I don't know . . . I'm just old school like that."

What's the Point?

We both paused for a while . . . I drove through a few streets on may way to an appointment, the silence between George and me opening up the dull rumble of the car along the pavement. George, once again, had nailed it. Writing as an art is a process of inspiration. As I've attempted to write throughout this little collection of thoughts, art comes out of a life spiritually attuned to God. The objective is not to produce words, but to draw close to God, to enter into loving union with God, and, out of that inspiration from the Holy Spirit, the writing emerges.

An AI, no matter how 'intelligent', cannot produce art. It wasn't created with a soul. It wasn't endowed with what humans are endowed with: the ability to be in union with God and to become divine beings. George, as usual—so annoying!—was right.

"You know man . . ." I cut in through the lingering silence, "you've just exposed how seduced I became by that technology! And that's just the whole problem with modernity anyway: that we place a premium on speed and output rather than on process."

"Well, and even deeper than that is our lives not being centred on writing and creating art but on loving God and all creation—output, production, 'art' are secondary. A tool like GPT shifts the focus back on production, on mass production, and speed; and no matter what you input, the AI is doing the producing. It's just the wrong focus, that's all. When we direct our lives to serving Christ and all people, then we're orientated the right way. And whether we create art or not, it doesn't really matter. I'm not saying we shouldn't create art. I'm just saying the focus of our lives must be on loving union with God."

As I complete this chapter, snapping away at the typewriter and trying not to disturb my family all sleeping in on a Saturday morning, I realize that this too, this Underwood 310, is a technology that at one point in history was groundbreaking in speeding up the writing process—I get it. And I also understand the extent to which I use technology every day, and that the 'term' technology from the Greek word 'techne' can mean broadly how one uses things to a particular goal. So I'm not trying to say that technology is in itself 'bad' (whatever that would mean);

but what I'm challenging is the seduction of some of these technological tools that are doing more and more of the thinking and producing for us. As George asked, "Where is the product coming from?" Topics like AI and the creation of art are highly contentious. And they'll become more contentious as the technology develops along its trajectory towards what Ray Kurzweil has for decades dubbed 'The Singularity', namely the integration of artificial intelligence with human intelligence thus creating supreme beings, or what Peter Diamandis calls 'gods', but I digress . . .

Nevertheless, the important thing is to be real, which means understanding the motivations and intent for creating art, and what the process is. The way I understand 'art' is that it comes from a heart that is working, struggling to be attuned to God. Human beings are embodied spirits. When we create art, we receive inspiration from God. The goal is not the writing itself. The writing is only one way to the goal, which is entering into loving union with God. Profficiency, speed, and productivity are therefore not the goal. And having a machine do the thinking and writing for me isn't the way either.

"Let them have their AI," George mused, "and we'll struggle to create real writing."

17
LIVING POETICALLY
WHAT A COMPOSER, A PRIEST, AND A SAINT ARE TEACHING ME ABOUT CREATIVITY

Living a poetic life is indeed for everyone—not just writers and painters and composers. St Porphyrios says that poetic hearts embrace love and sense it deeply.

O LORD my God, you are very great; You are clothed with honour and majesty, Who cover Yourself with light as with a garment, Who stretch out the heavens like a curtain. Psalm 104

Arvo Pärt

To pursue Beauty, Goodness, and Truth is to live poetically. And to live poetically is not an orientation exclusive to artists, writers, and painters. To live poetically is the life of one who is truly human, truly alive, truly present, and open to God, neighbour, and creation. One artistic example who has inspired me is Arvo Pärt.

In a master class by composer Arvo Pärt on his composition *Spiegel im Spiegel*, Pärt reflects on the importance of each note.

> A need to concentrate on each sound, so that every blade of grass would be as important as a flower. It could be like a break on the radio. Such signals sometimes sound as if they lasted an entire life. Or future, or past, outside time. Like I said: a blade of grass has the status of a flower. To see in this tiny phrase something more than just the black and white key . . . It's not the tune that matters so much here . . it's the combination the triad that makes such a heart-rending union. The soul yearns to sing it endlessly.

To compose a single note with as much care as one would gaze at and admire a flower; but then to see a simple blade of grass holding as much value . . . to care for each word, each note . . . to hold a blade of grass in your hand and know it and love it. I heard one say that if you want to learn to draw simply sit and stare at a blade of grass long enough to draw it. If you can draw a blade of grass, you can draw anything.

The Cosmology of Poetic Living

Indeed Pärt's love for the single note and the blade of grass is reminiscent of Father Lev Gillet and St Porphyrios. St Porphyrios writes this piece of inspiration in his book *Wounded by Love*:

> Love is limitless in space. Have you ever read the 104th Psalm? In the Orthodox Church it is said every evening at the beginning of Vespers . . . In it the whole universe passes by the mountains and the sea, the wind and the storms, the wild beasts and the humblest little animals, the trees and the rocks. It is a whole cosmology, which ought to guide our piety towards avenues far wider than any 'private' relationship with God. What we need to do is let ourselves be carried away by the immense current

> of Limitless Love by that impulse that progression of all of nature which according to Saint Paul waits liberation from the consequences of the Fall. Nevertheless we must beware lest any ascent of man towards God obscures for us the descent of God towards man.[1]

Father Lev Gillet shows us the cosmological nature of our relationship with God. We raise our minds, our hearts, our groaning, our praises to God as all of creation does, from the greatest galaxy to the smallest humble creature, and even the blade of grass.

> Take a flower in your hand, take a stone, ponder upon them, not from the scientific angle of the botanist or the geologist, but from the spiritual viewpoint. Each of them is an epitome of the evolution of the world towards the total Christ of whom Saint Paul speaks.[2]

As Christ the Logos, the underlying Principle and Order of all that is, the flower, the stone point back to the Word that wrought them, and ahead to their culmination in the new heaven and earth. Far from 'mere matter' the flower, the stone, the grass blade point us to Christ.

> They are also signs of Love coming towards us, revealing itself to us, giving itself to us, coming ever closer and closer. Gaze on the divine beauty in a blade of grass in a leaf, in a branch. Perceive an offering in a scent, in a colour. Let us integrate our spiritual lives with the life of the universe. Let us recognize in every creature a spring of divine Love fitting to itself, and to itself alone. The lord Love has loved each grain of sand, each stone, each leaf, each shrub, each animal.[3]

To live poetically is more than just 'being present' for the blade of grass or flower; it is to see the Lord Love loving all of it. It is connected to Christ through a 'presencing with' nature around me. To not only see something beautiful, but to see it as loved deeply by God. And then to enter it:

> To unite ourselves to all this, to enter into that great rising and falling tide of love to adore God and to give thanks to Him in the name of nature (which cannot speak)—this is 'cosmic piety'. This is our reply to Limitless Love.[4]

Surrounded by nature, we can enter into it and there find Love Himself. Art then arises from the soul that loves the Beautiful and seeks to create out of that union with the cosmos and draw others into it.

> Do you love the sun? Do you love the stars? Do you love the galaxies? Do you thank God for their creation and for their presence? Do you enter into divine Love for all that exists? Perhaps this is difficult for you.[5]

It isn't easy . . . What is easy is to take it all for granted; to drink up the world, wipe our lips, and seek insatiably for more. Once consumed, it's harder to offer it back to God in love.

Hugged a Tree Lately?

Have you ever hugged or kissed or venerated a tree as you would an icon or the Bible or Cross? Offering a blessing to the tree, giving thanks for it, acknowledging its blessedness before God, its place in the universe in time and space. Trees, grass, rocks, the cosmos become friends. The world is ours, created for our enjoyment. But it is also there for us to love, to hug, to kiss, to offer up in thanksgiving. This is one of the ways I like to a affirm my identity as a 'priest' and affirm the earth as sacred before God. But what about the beasts that scare us, like spiders and creepy crawlies and snakes? Father Lev Gillet:

> Do you love snakes? But even if we are bitten by a snake we ought to be able to love it at the very moment when we were bitten because the snake is not to blame, it is simply obeying an imperative of its instinct. The snake, like all nature, has been a victim of the Fall, but the Lord Love has not ceased to love it.[6]

What I take from Fr Lev Gillet is to enter into even what scares me and trust in the love of God, that I am His child. The more I enter into the Beauty of the love of God, that loving union, the more my heart will be changed, softened, so that even if I am bitten by a snake or attacked by a bear I can forgive them.

There is something about the cosmic piety of Fr Lev Gillet refers to and living poetically or creatively that really strikes me; there is a connectedness to the earth that we have because Christ the Logos dwells within us, and within it. We can live poetically—not only intellectually, but also ontologically, namely a poetic life that is lived not merely in our heads, not only in concept, but in our very being, in the experiences of our lives, in the deepest places of our hearts.

St Porphyrios also writes beautifully about living poetically. In his book *Wounded by Love*, the blessed saint writes about a "poetical life" while revealing to us how he lives.

> Flowers for example have their own grace: they teach us with their fragrance and with their magnificence. They speak to us of the love of God. They scatter their

> fragrance and their beauty on sinners and on the righteous.[7]

Living poetically is seeing Christ everywhere and in all things, filling all things, loving all things, and entering into union with that Love.

Cultivate a Poetic Soul

St Porphyrios wrote about the importance of cultivating a poetic soul; a soul that is open to Beauty, Goodness, and Truth in creation, to see God's energies, His grace, in everything and give thanks for it.

> For a person to become a Christian he must have a poetic soul. He must become a poet. Christ does not wish insensitive souls in His company. A Christian, albeit only when he loves, is a poet and lives amid poetry. Poetic hearts embrace love and sense it deeply.[8]

A misunderstanding would be to believe that only writers can live poetically. To live such a blessed poetic life is for all Christians—as St Porphyrios writes above, the Christian must become a poet. I believe what he is saying is that we live poetically when we love, when our hearts embrace love and sense it deeply. A love that sees every person, every living thing as filled with the glory of God, gives thanks for it, and honours and cherishes it.

This kind of embracing love is for all of us. To be human is to be open to the love of God all around us. To see ourselves placed in a world of order and beauty. To know that we are in the hands of a loving God at all times. That in the same way He looks after plants, trees, and animals, so even more is He looking after me. Because as a Christian I affirm Christ the Logos, I also affirm His creation. I thus see myself as part of His creation, not set over against it. Living poetically is also an awareness of my own being-with the cosmos. To see that I belong to a greater interconnected and fully alive natural and spiritual world, which is greater than my own little life.

Living poetically moves me into making the most of the present moment, to find its inherent beauty and affirm it and thank God for it. St Porphyrios says that when we are aware of beauty in the present moment, our souls become predisposed to prayer. That beautiful moments "make the soul refined, noble, and poetic."[9] We then begin to see the presence of God in everything:

> When a lovely landscape, a picturesque chapel, or something beautiful inspires you, don't leave things at that, but go beyond this to give glory for all beautiful things so that you can experience Him who alone is comely in beauty. All things are holy—the sea, swimming and eating. Take delight in them all. All things enrich us, all lead us to the Great Love. All lead us to Christ.[10]

What becomes clear to me when I read this passage is just how much St Porphyrios lived that kind of poetic life—and still does. There is a presence of heaven that we can experience here on earth: to see everything as holy, sacred, held together by the love of God. To delight in life, this life, this present moment; to offer it up to God in thanksgiving. Thanksgiving opens me to that heavenly realm regardless of the circumstance. Like the Thanksgiving Prayer: "We thank you for everything, concerning everything, and in everything . . ." To create art, to write well, requires that I live my life more and more in this presence and Beauty; to see the grace of God, His energies, in everything, and to be open to the sacredness of the world, nature, my wife, my children, my family and friends, and every other human I meet; to venerate trees and plants; to look at animals with love; to walk along God's earth and witness heaven. This is the way I need to try to be open to God, to catch a glimpse of the world in its fullness and nakedness at the same time: as holy and vulnerable—resplendent yet fully reliant on God. To see the world in a simple way; to stand in its openness and see things as they are—to see things with the eyes of Love and see them all as icons of Christ.

Become Like a Child

To live poetically is to explore and learn to be childlike. This is difficult for me sometimes because I can be driven to seriousness and rigidity out of fear or insecurity. When I am like this, the world looks grey and morose, like I'm stuck in a Morissey song: that dull seaside tourist town. But children can be so full of gaiety and wonder, so into just experiencing the world. They are keen to seeing how things work. They are not yet curmudgeonly old cynics. They ask questions out of wonder, not out of deconstruction. And they care about what's around them. I need to become more like that. St Porphyrios urges us to observe everything around us with a sense of wonder—houses, buildings, towns, villages, people and their civilizations. And that we must ask questions to enrich our understanding about each and every thing, big or small. And not to be indifferent, smug, or cynical. Such an orientation to the world "makes you meditate more deeply on the wonders of God. All things become an opportunity to join more closely with everything and everyone."[11]

How much is modern society that kind of indifference to everything around us? I stare at my phone, look up for a moment, stare back at it. Scroll through social media video feeds while on a boat skipping across a beautiful vast lake, or mediate the boating trip through the phone by taking a video of myself before uploading it immediately waiting for all the likes to appear. Stare down, stare up for a moment, stare down again. Nothing interesting but the endless scroll and the insatiable desire to see and be truly seen. St Porphyrios is calling me to look up—to be attentive. To put the phone away and take delight not only in the natural world but also in the manufactured world; to allow the ingenuity of human beings to inspire me. To take notice. To be interested. To talk to people around me and ask questions, rather stand in silent judgment and critique. To enter dialogue with all its risk and encounter and messiness. This it seems is part of living poetically. Living in this way brings us closer to thanksgiving, to repentance, and therefore to God. And for St Porphyrios, it leads to a different way of seeing, a way of seeing the essence of things.

> The man who has the Spirit of God is attentive wherever he passes by; he is all eyes, all senses of smell. All his senses are alert in the Spirit of God. He is different. He sees everything and hears everything: he sees the stone, the birds, the butterfly . . . When he walks by somewhere, he senses each thing, a fragrance for example.[12]

The one who lives poetically is fully present and fully alive. There is no leaving the present moment—or what would refer to as despondency—but to be fully open to it. When I live poetically, I see the Spirit of God and Christ Himself in everything. I become "all eyes and sense of smell."

How often do I want this aliveness but am too caught up in my own thoughts and schedules and text messages to realize? Sometimes I find myself in the midst of a forest or mountain and don't realize till I've left that not once was I aware of the presence of God. What about the blade of grass curling out from between two sidewalk stones? . . . St Porphyrios:

> [The poet] lives amidst everything—the butterflies, the bees, and so on. Grace makes him attentive. He wishes to be together with all things.[13]

This is how we can cultivate a poetic soul, how we can become poets and how we can live poetically. And what strikes me about this orientation to the world is that it is not a mere means to a creative end—we don't do things so we can become more creative, to 'get a handle' on things or be 'dialled in'. Rather, we enter into life, our experiences authentically as ones created in the image and likeness of God. And out of that identity we live as poets, as artists, to express the beauty and struggle of our existence, and ultimately to dwell in the presence of God who is everywhere and filling all things.

18

OPENING THE SOUL TO GOD

THE BEAUTY AND PAIN OF CONFESSIONAL WRITING

Confessional writing is the opening of the soul to God and to others through prose. This chapter focuses on examples of confessional writing for inspiration.

Out of the depths I cry to You, O Lord! O Lord, hear my voice! Let Your ears be attentive to the voice of my pleas for mercy! Psalm 130

How Could I?

Some of my favourite writing is confessional prose and autobiographical fiction. There are the obvious examples that are actual confessions like St Augustine's or St Patrick's *Confessions.* Then there are other forms of literary confessions that are more or less evident.

Czeslaw Milosz is an example of one whose poetry tends towards veiled confession, for he was a writer who sought to live and work as a poet not as a reporter. He thus sought to live in a way that allows us, in Milosz's own words, "to acquire the perspective that lets us contemplate the things in this world without delusions," which for him "acquired a religious dimension" having been raised as a Catholic.[1] His poem *How Could I?* expresses this clarity of contemplation.

> How could I
> Do such things
> Living in this hideous world Subject to
> its laws
> Toying with its laws.
> I need God, so that He may forgive me
> I need a God of mercy.[2]

Karl Ove Knausgård is another example of autobiographical fiction. His writing is so confessional that he and the protagonist of his books blur into one another. One set of books he wrote are titled *Min Kamp*, or *My Confession*. His books are so true to nature that a number of his relationships have been sacrificed for his writing—an outcome or consequence he simply accepts. He stated in an interview with his estranged wife Tonje Aursland, who plays a part in several of Knausgård's *Min Kamp* books, that sometimes he feels he has made a "Faustian bargain"—that he has achieved huge success by sacrificing his relationships with friends and members of his family. When reading Knausgård I am periodically reminded of Woody Allen's tragicomic film *Deconstructing Harry* in which the protagonist is perpetually harassed—even threatened—by the characters of his books coming back to haunt him as relationships in real life. For Knausgård, such backlash is simply the unintended consequences of his art.

> The only genres I saw value in, which still conferred meaning, were diaries and essays, the types of literature that did not deal with narrative, that were not about anything, but just consisted of a voice, the voice of your

> own personality, a life, a face, a gaze you could meet. What is a work of art if not the gaze of another person? Not directed above us, nor beneath us, but at the same height as our own gaze. Art cannot be experienced collectively, nothing can. Art is something you are alone with. You meet its gaze alone.[3]

Look at all the writing on social media—people pouring their hearts out, writing near tomes on the first-world struggles of their lives. And how many people read it? Many. Though not as polished or well-crafted as literature (in most cases), such spontaneous acts of confessional writing points to something deep inside us: the desire to be seen, not just at our best, but at our worst. That's probably why I like confessional writing so much. It's raw and real. It's not fluffed up. It betrays the fallenness of the human being and his desire to reveal it as a way to somehow move beyond it towards redemption. That's what makes us human: the desire to move beyond our transgressions to wholeness and healing, even if we fail miserably in the process.

The Fig Tree

Ted Hughes was married for a time to poet Sylvia Plath. Plath was a sort of pioneer of modern confessional poetry. This excerpt from her book *Bell Jar* is disturbing and painful and poignant.

> I saw my life branching out before me like the green fig tree in the story. From the tip of every branch, like a fat purple fig, a wonderful future beckoned and winked. One fig was a husband and a happy home and children, and another fig was a famous poet and another fig was a brilliant professor, and another fig was Ee Gee, the amazing editor, and another fig was Europe and Africa

> and South America, and another fig was Constantin and Socrates and Attila and a pack of other lovers with queer names and off-beat professions, and another fig was an Olympic lady crew champion, and beyond and above these figs were many more figs I couldn't quite make out. I saw myself sitting in the crotch of this fig tree, starving to death, just because I couldn't make up my mind which of the figs I would choose. I wanted each and every one of them, but choosing one meant losing all the rest, and, as I sat there, unable to decide, the figs began to wrinkle and go black, and, one by one, they plopped to the ground at my feet.[4]

What terrifying imagery—the image of wanting everything and letting it all rot before you! And yet how poignant and telling and transparent this image; how Plath takes us to this fig tree and points out the various figs, and names each one. We stand there with her in the crotch of the tree under an abundance of fruit, which in many ways is also representative of our lives. And under the sun of a summer day, the sky filled with so much hope and opportunity, rather than offer it all to God in thanksgiving, we are sick with an overwhelming lust to consume it all in the midst of which we freeze as the fruit one by one blackens and falls rotten before us, and before the one who has led us here, the poet, the confessor, Sylvia Plath.

In poet Ted Hughes's *Paris Review* interview, he speaks in some detail about his short time with Plath, her suicide, and the decision he made as her benefactor to not release her journals to the public. He also shares his understanding of confessional writing. He talks about the plausibility that all poetry is "revealing something that the writer doesn't actually want to say but desperately needs to communicate, to be delivered of."[5] The tension of revealing and concealing is what makes the writing poetic, makes it poetry. "The writer," Hughes continues, "daren't actually put it into words, so it leaks out obliquely, smuggled through analogies. We think we're writing to amuse, but we're actually saying something we desperately need to share."[6] This desperation to share builds up and becomes a kind of poetic or literary confession that Hughes finds exasperating: "Why can't we just hide it and shut up? Why do we have to blab? Why do human beings need to confess?" Then he resigns himself to the following conclusion:

> Maybe if you don't have a secret confession, you don't have a poem—don't even have a story. Don't have a writer . . . [Until] the revelation's actually published, the poet feels no release.[7]

The desire or need of the writer to confess to a public audience might partly be remnants of a common practice (prior to one confessing solely to a priest) in which people confessed their sins before the entire church congregation. Another offshoot of this is the phenomenon of public testimony in churches everywhere during which one tells their story to a group of people about their past (typically graphically 'sinful') with their acceptance of or return to Christ. Alcoholics and drug addicts have no problem confessing their sins— they know themselves very well, how broken they are, and how much help they need. In contrast, the more 'successful' one appears, the more difficult it is for them to confess—their clothes, cars, and upstanding position in society are the armour they have built around themselves as protection from public scrutiny. And perhaps this is why such confessional writers are so important: they become the medium between the reader and their sins;

that in reading the confession of the writer, they are in essence confessing through them.

Life Becomes Art

Søren Kierkegaard wrote in a similar way. Just look at one of his most famous pieces of writing: *Diary of a Seducer*, found in one of his first works entitled *Either/Or*. In *Diary of a Seducer*, the protagonist leads on a young girl only to break up with her shortly after their engagement. In this story, Kierkegaard was revealing his broken engagement with Regina Olson, while providing the occasion for the reader to see his or her own self in the seducer's confession of betrayal. In fact, Kierkegaard gives the reader a hint about his two-way confessional method with the epigraph of *Either/Or*:

> My books are like a mirror: if a monkey looks in, a saint can't look back out.

Kierkegaard, in addition to a number of groundbreaking books, left behind a trove of journals which give us an occasion to peer behind the philosopher and his seemingly nebulous prose into Kierkegaard's often morose and ruminating thoughts, his deep existential struggles and pain. This particular excerpt has been one of my favourites for years.

> What I really need is to get clear about what I must do, not what I must know, except insofar as knowledge must precede every act. What matters is to find a purpose, to see what it really is that God wills that I shall do; the crucial thing is to find a truth which is truth for me, to find the idea for which I am willing to live and die.[8]

And another …

> I have just now come from a party where I was its life and soul; witticisms streamed from my lips, everyone laughed and admired me but I went away—yes, the dash should be as long as the radius of the earth's orbit-------------------and wanted to shoot myself.[9]

While studying writers like Kierkegaard in university, some of my professors warned against the fallacy of psychologizing, that is, reading an author's personal life into his or her prose. And yet without fail in those instances in which I interpreted their writing in the context of their biography I could gain valuable insights, for from what other experiences do we draw from in writing? The confessional or autobiographical writer makes those connections more explicit. They pull you into their nebulous world of sin, into the toxicity of their thoughts. Their honesty is painful. Part of reading a confessional writer's prose is hoping that they will find light, or glorying in their finding it, or upon reading about their attainment of some kind of virtue hoping it for ourselves.

We are all sinners, and thus all confessors in one way or another. This is why perhaps I am attracted to confessional writing so much: part of me marvels at the ability of the writer to bare his or her soul on the page, the other part of me wishes I could have the freedom and unbridled vulnerability to do the same. That said, there is a gift that confessional writing can provide: that my life can become an offering for another to read and resonate with and be edified by—perhaps even find their way to God. In confessional writing our lives, our pasts, our failures, our joys and pains are no longer ours but used by God for others.

19
FROM CURSE TO GIFT
WHY WE SHOULD NEVER FEAR WRITER'S BLOCK

Writer's block is considered worse than terminal illness. But perhaps there's more to it than that. Maybe your writer's block is a gift from God.

Have mercy on me, O LORD, for I am weak; O LORD, heal me, for my bones are troubled. My soul also is greatly troubled; But You, O LORD—how long? Psalm 6:2

Writer's Block a Gift??

I was listening to a lecture by Father Stephen Freeman. During the talk, he said something that made my back straighten up. He said, in that way only Father Stephen Freeman can say it: "Ya know . . . sometimes God gives us writer's block as a gift." As a gift?

I shook my head and turned up the volume to hear more while also wanting to call Fr Stephen immediately and personally interrogate him further: Isn't writer's block a bad thing? Isn't writer's block the bane of the writer? Isn't writer's block worse than the most vile terminal illness?

Scores of books have been written to help people through the devastation of writer's block—two excellent ones, for example, are Julia Cameron's *The Artist's Way,* and the brash, in your face book by Stephen Pressfield, still one of my absolute favourites, *The War of Art.* Writer's block, for Cameron and Pressfield is the scourge of writers that needs to be destroyed—period. And I mean look at Rainer Maria Rilke! How long did his writer's block last? Thirteen years or more? Who wants writer's block, seriously!

But contrary to those and many other sources around creativity and the creative process, maybe writer's block is a good thing; maybe it is a gift from God—at least that's Fr Stephen's point.

The Art of Writing Without Writing

I have a friend who's a writer. He's written several books, and has been an active writer every day for as long as I've known him. He came to me one day to tell me that he didn't know what was happening but that he had not been actively writing for almost a year.

"What do you mean you haven't been writing?" I asked.

"I haven't been writing anything substantial—" he replied, "no books, manuscripts, articles, nothing."

"But what about your routine? Haven't you been following your routine?"

"My routine is gone . . . I have no routine anymore. I used to get up in the morning and pray then write for at least an hour. But for whatever reason, I haven't been able to write."

"So what do you do?" I asked surprised by this shift in my friend's routine. I mean he's had that thing locked in for years. How could it have changed?

"I've been focusing more on prayer . . . The writing has just slipped into the background and I'm not going to push it. It seems forced to give myself only a certain amount of time to pray then heed the alarm and switch gears to sit down and write. Prayer has taken over. Right now, I'd rather stand before the icons in stillness. I prefer silence to sitting down to write. It's changed for me—I don't know what else to say."

"Do you see yourself going back to writing?" I was dumbfounded.

"Well I've got some projects I'm thinking about but there's no urgency right now. Maybe I just need to be quiet and do nothing for a while. Maybe this is something I need to accept and not fight. Maybe the writing can wait . . . I don't know . . . it's never happened to me before . . . not like this."

As I reflected on my conversation with my friend, I could see something else was going on in his life. I could see that what he was engaged in wasn't the classic understanding of writer's block, but rather he was in a process of entering deeper into prayer. He was putting God before the writing. He was recentring, realigning his soul with his true Source of Life, with Life Himself. He was making room in his heart for God. He was opening himself to what God wanted to do in his life through this seeming gift of writer's block. I wanted to know more.

"So what does prayer look like to you then these days? I mean, how have you been substituting writing for prayer?

"Sometimes I sit, sometimes I pray the hours, sometimes I make prostrations—I don't know. One thing I do know is I'm not writing at that usual time."

"But you're not freaked out? I mean . . . that's a huge shift for you. Aren't you afraid of . . . you know . . . (gulp) . . . writer's block?" I could hardly get the last two words out —it's my nightmare too.

"I was for a while, thinking I was a total failure. If I'm a writer, how can I not be writing? And if I'm not writing, how can I call myself a writer? But that's a bad track of thought. 'Writer' is not my identity—at least, that's what I'm learning through all of this. Maybe the mask is burning away, and I'm finding out who I am before God —you know . . . His kid. And when I look at myself, at my identity like that, then maybe I won't get so depressed when the writing isn't coming hot off the pen."

The Poison as the Remedy

It was here that Fr Stephen's comment about God's gift of writer's block struck a chord with my conversation with my friend: That what to the world appeared to be a disease was actually a kind of medicine; a way for God to refocus our attention, to sharpen our vision, to bring us as writers into a deeper encounter with Him, to ensure that we are doing our work for the right reason and in the right manner. That in the hands of God writer's block is a gift of healing. Healing from what? Pride, ego, self-reliance, self-actualization—all the selfie diseases that take us down faster than a bottle of Jack Daniels. All the things the 'creativity gurus' tell us we need to have to become a success —that strong sense of self, and all manner of self obsession. For my friend, he saw his writer's block as a journey into greater freedom, into becoming more of his true self. "For," he said to me, "I'd rather be a failure in the world's eyes and God's kid than some kind of banal representation of success."

As I reflected on my conversation with my friend—on my own fear of writer's block, on the crazy notion of writer's block as a gift—I thought of two things. First, I thought of the quote by St Pope Kyrillos VI when he said, "All I have is Yours." And second, I was taken to the Thanksgiving Prayer from the Divine Liturgy of St Basil:

> We give thanks for what is Yours,
> For everything, Concerning everything,
> And in everything.

Even writer's block! Fr Stephen Freeman is right: Glory to God for all things!

20

IN SEARCH OF LOST TIME

ART AND THE WAY OF LOVING STILLNESS

Sometimes we get down by how little we've produced. But instead of trying to produce more, we can take time and be still and say a little prayer to God or ask the intercession of St Mary or our patron saint. To turn off the ruminating mind, and be still.

He shall be like a tree planted by the rivers of water, that brings forth its fruit in its season, whose leaf also shall not wither; and whatever he does shall prosper.
Psalm 1:3

The Despair of Productivity

I was struck by this quote by Dostoevsky:

> When I look back on my past and think how much time I wasted on nothing, how much time has been lost in futilities, errors, laziness, incapacity to live; how little I appreciated it, how many times I sinned against my heart and soul then my heart bleeds. Life is a gift, life is

> happiness, every minute can be an eternity of happiness.[1]

A sense of lost time or wasted time can lead to despair. In a world that pushes the drugs of ambition and success, that's all about climbing the ladder, there can be a lot of regret and resentment when it comes to our past. Sometimes the antidote is to write or create through the despair. But other times it might mean doing nothing at all, and turning to the present moment. This excerpt from the words of Zossima in *The Brothers Karamazov* provides an antidote to the pain of wasted time:

> Love animals, love the plants, love everything. If you love everything, you will perceive the divine mystery in things. Once you perceive it you will begin to comprehend it better every day. And you will come at last to love the whole world with an all-embracing love.[2]

This is the orientation of the true artist in response to sloth and sluggishness and wasted time. Despair wants to bring me into myself, into sloth and despondency—to make me believe that only my thoughts exist. I become a temporary solipsist, namely that I am the only one who exists in the world. But the reality is that I dwell in a world that is created out of love and was deemed by God to be exceedingly beautiful. To enter the beauty of the world is this: to see the world as it truly is which is the perspective of art. And this is why I think St Porphyrios encourages us to become poets; for to become poets is to see the world poetically, that is in all of its beauty. This perspective, this way, is to see with the eyes of Love. Why? Because God created the world out of love. To see the world this way is to see the world through the eyes of love and thus in the way it was created.

The Look

When I am open to the world through the eyes of love my perception of others changes too. My apprehension of the beauty of the created world opens me to the beauty found in each person, the image of God in each person. And when I see God in each person, I am less prone to judge them. Father Seraphim Rose advises, "Don't criticize or judge other people," and, instead, "regard everyone else as an angel, justify their mistakes and weaknesses, and condemn only yourself as the worst sinner."[3] For this is the path to the spiritual life.

Looking at others through the eyes of love, and letting myself be loved by God through repentance and a desire for meekness and humility, is the way; it is what I am created to become, for this is the way I, and all of us, have been created. Seeing everyone as those who bear the image of God and loving them is the purpose, the goal, of human life. It is how we recover from the hardness and cruelty and sanctimoniousness of the fallen world, and find our true selves and become who we are. To gaze at the world out of love, and to see the entire cosmos and its myriad beings as they truly are, is to see with the eyes of non-attachment, which St John Climacus in the *Ladder of Divine Ascent* calls "renunciation." It is to renounce the ego that seeks to cling to and use the world for its own desires, to drink up the entire world and desire more —always more! To offer the world to myself rather than back to God in thanksgiving, and thus short circuit the natural harmony of myself, God, my neighbour, and the natural world. St John Climacus advises us instead to be like those "who sit outside the city amongst the tombs," and pray silently and continually, "with fiery streams of tears and voiceless heartfelt groaning" until Christ appears to us, and, as He did with Lazarus, rolls away the stone of hardness from our hearts, and looses us from the bonds of sin and the passions.[4] Only then can we begin to see the world and others as they truly are.

The Way of Renunciation

Renunciation is hard. I love the world too much—its pleasures, its nostalgia, its tastes and music and rhythms. To renounce the world, to not only turn away from it but profess a turning away from it, leads to a kind of bitter sorrow and despair. To renounce the world is to give up what I once thought was my home, my identity, everything I was taught growing up—the customs and conventions of 'normal' western life. But sometimes I find myself in situations that provide a glimpse into how fake the world really is, how trite, how painfully dull and boring, how cold and meaningless the constant pursuit of more and more really is; how corrupt and brutal and unjust its systems of power and oppression are; how manipulative the whole mass media industry is; how in the smallest way my tastes, my memories, my beliefs have been shaped by multinational companies and supranational entities that only seek my compliance and cowardice.

I realize that what I knew as 'western civilization' has been a fabrication, a set of narratives and beliefs that loosely hang together and pull at the seams under any honest process of analysis and scrutiny. How my identity as a GenXer has been made up for me, including my seeming 'love' for Pearl Jam and Morrisey and Coca Cola. That the perspiring nausea I experienced at the mall and golf courses and dinner parties and corporate functions, anything that involved social etiquette, was a tell tale sign that there was a more authentic way to live and I was far from it.

These kinds of experiences leading us to despair and cynicism reveal a hunger for life as it truly is, which involves renouncing everything that makes it fake and obligatory and dull and nauseating. And, if we are led in the right way, such experiences and the revelation of such a hunger can lead us to renunciation of the world and a desire for Beauty, Goodness, and Truth. At such a point, we wish to 'get real' and enter a different Way, the Way of Christ. I continue to marvel at how many these days are realizing that they've been sold a bill of goods—intellectually, creativity, spiritually, politically—that, once the initial thrill has worn off, the veneer of value, they have been left with nothing but meaninglessness and despair. And then they start asking different questions that lead to a definitive spiritual path, a Way—the Way Himself—that we have been created for, and their lives completely change.

Silent Before the Icons

Maybe there are times when writing and producing take back seat to just being. Maybe the best way to deal with the resentment of sloth and laziness in a world obsessed with action and success and constant hits of dopamine, is not to do anything at all, but simply sit by the icons and be silent and still.

One person who wrote a lot about his resentment and despair in the midst of a culture obsessed with success and accomplishment and action is Henri Nouwen. A marked experience in his life, at a time of fatigue and brokenness, was when on a retreat at a monastery someone placed in his room an icon of Rublev's Feast of the Holy Trinity. In his little gem of a book entitled *Behold the Beauty of the Lord: Praying with Icons*, Nouwen shares with us the importance that just sitting with icons in silent prayer has been a gift at times when he could do nothing much more than that. It began at a period in his life, he describes, "in which verbal prayer had become nearly impossible and during which mental and emotional fatigue had made me the easy victim of feelings of despair and fear . . ." Rublev's icon had been placed in Nouwen's room, the "long and quiet presence" of which "became the beginning of my healing. As I sat for long hours in front of Rublev's Trinity, I noticed how gradually my gaze became my prayer. This silent prayer slowly made my inner restlessness melt away and lifted me up into the circle of love, a circle that could not be broken by the powers of the world."[5]

Sometimes there is nothing more than I can do but just sit there gazing up at Mama (St Mary), our Lord Jesus Christ, St Moses the Strong, St Mary of Egypt, St Patrick . . . to just stare up at them, their halos radiant in candle light, their silent presence, their glory, and just be with them realizing I have nothing to offer, nothing to give but the will to enter their presence, the Kingdom of Heaven, and by grace dwell with them. To experience how tired I am, the failure and vapidness of words, the flood of ruminating thoughts, my lack of anything I can offer to God but a very broken desire to just be with Him. I thus can resonate with how Rublev's icon became for Nouwen the beginning of his healing, and how his long gazes at the icon became his prayer, his prayer from the depths of his heart that was beyond words. And that his desire for healing and wholeness and unity for himself, for his friends, for the entire world—as he wrote so extensively about—was met by the Beauty, the Goodness, the Truth of the Holy Trinity everywhere present and filling all things, restoring all things, healing all things, bringing the cosmos back into order through Christ's Incarnation, His baptism, His miracles and teachings, His death, resurrection, and ascension, through His Church, through our prayers, through our feeble actions, through the work of the saints, His blessed and holy Mother and the heavenly hosts, through the Love and grace and holiness of God Himself. Nouwen describes this state of being "lifted up into the circle of love that could not be broken by the powers of the world." Hence Nouwen observed that for him "the contemplation of [Rublev's icon of the Trinity] has increasingly become a way to enter more deeply into the mystery of divine life while remaining fully engaged in the struggles of our hate-and-fear-filled world."[6]

Entering into Beauty

As writers and artists, as simple Christians, sometimes we feel this is the best we can do: stand before God in prayer. Then perhaps over time we begin to realize this is the only thing worthwhile for us to do in the first place. What's the goal of our creating anyway? To be productive? Successful? Ambitious? Or to grow in loving union with God, to become more like Him, to become saints? And maybe before we create poetry, or become poets, we need to begin to see the world as deeply and richly beautiful, which begins by learning to sit and be present and still and silent and seek an encounter with God; to enter deeply into His Beauty.

Seeking to enter loving union with God sounds easy in a book or on paper—and perhaps it should be. It should perhaps be easy and light for our souls to enter into loving union with the One who created and sustains life. But there are many days when it is the hardest thing for me to do—mostly because of my ego, my false assumptions about what this encounter should 'look' or 'feel' like. And it's hard to just sit and 'be' when I feel like a total failure for not producing anything, or people don't read my books. But these are moments that can open me to strength and courage and healing—this practice that has been an essential part of the Orthodox Christian faith for millennia of sitting in silence and stillness before God, and receiving from Him succour for our pain and despair; and to believe that the greatest advances we can make is by just sitting quietly with Him.

However, sometimes those moments of sitting quietly in stillness can trigger further resentments, failures, and all the ways I've fallen short. In such times I need to ask God for a renewal of my eyes so I can actually see the Beauty that is ever and all around me, and just continue to sit in His Love and apprehend it all, giving myself fully into that Beauty and letting my soul be healed and nourished by the One Who is He and He alone.

21

WHAT IS THE MOST IMPORTANT THING?

A MONK'S ENCOUNTER WITH THE THEOTOKOS

Creativity is a gift from God. But sometimes all of us lose sight of the purpose of the Way—the goal, the direction: to become saints.

He shall be like a tree planted by the rivers of water, that brings forth its fruit in its season, whose leaf also shall not wither; and whatever he does shall prosper.
Psalm 1:3

Everyday Saints

As human beings, we are creative in many ways—it's one of the gifts God has given us. And we seek to do all sorts of things with the gift of creativity—indeed many things. In this orientation to the creative life, it's easy to get busy and lose sight of the goal or objective—the true goal or objective—of our lives.

One of my favourite books is about the Pskov Monastery in Russia and the monks who live there, entitled *Everyday Saints*. There are many intriguing, inspiring—even hilarious—stories in this book. But one story, a simple story, really struck me, particularly as it relates to creativity and the incessant craving for creating more that we all have—the drive to be productive. The monk writing the book, Archimandrite Tikhon, reflects on a time when he was assigned to vigil prayer from eleven o'clock until midnight. After his shift, a schema monk named Father Superior Melchizedek, would relieve him and read the Psalter until two o'clock in the morning. Archimandrite Tikhon reflects that "taking the monastic schema vows in the Russian Orthodox Church involves the very highest degree of ascetic withdrawal from the world. The monk who does this foregoes all other service and tasks except for prayer."[1]

Just before Father Melchizedek's shift, he "would always appear beneath the vaults of the small and dimly lit Church of St Lazarus, the place the Psalms were always read aloud unceasingly." He would stand at the Royal Doors and slowly bow three times as Father Tikhon would approach. Father Tikhon was taken aback by Father Melchizedek even though the latter never said an actual word to him. "I . . . understood how extraordinarily lucky I was to be able to simply see this remarkable ascetic every night—even if all I could do was simply look at him, but not speak to him."[2]

Words Spoken in the Dark

Finally Father Tikhon mustered up the courage to speak to Father Melchizedek—to finally ask him the one question that all the other novices and young monks of the monastery could dream of asking.

As a backstory, before Father Melchizedek had taken the great monastic schema, he was named Father Michael, and he was a great carpenter. He made icon frames, lecterns, chairs, tables, chests of drawers, and all kinds of furniture. He worked with great focus from dawn to dusk. One day he accepted a commission to make a very large and important piece for the monastery. He worked so hard that when he completed the work, he collapsed and died. Some of the monks rushed in to help him—Father Michael showed no signs of life. But one of the elder monks prayed over Father Michael and suddenly the latter opened his eyes and was revived. When Father Michael had been revived more fully, he asked the monks to summon the abbot to him. When the abbot arrived, Father Michael begged him to take the vows to enter the great monastic schema. The question Father Tikhon asked the now Father Melchizedek was why did he leave behind his carpentry and become a completely different person. What happened when he died? Father Melchizedek did not say a word for a long time—he just stood by the Royal Gates of the altar head hung low. After a while, he began to speak albeit in a voice grown weak from saying so few words.

All We Wanted was Just One Thing …

He describes standing in the middle of a giant field through which he began to walk without any sense of direction. After a while his path was blocked by a great mote. And sticking out of the mud Father Melchizedek saw all kinds of icon frames, church lecterns, and metal overlay for icons. Amidst all that were crooked tables, broken chairs, and wardrobes. The more he gazed at these things stuck in this mote, covered in mud and clumps of earth, the more he realized they were his own carpentry work. He then felt that someone was standing over his shoulder. Father Melchizedek lifted up his head and saw that it was the Mother of God: She was gazing with sorrow over all of Father Melchizedek's work.

Then she spoke:

> You are a monk . . . And all we wanted from you was just one thing: repentance and prayer. Instead of that, you gave us wood work.[3]

After St Mary spoke those words, the apparition vanished. The dead man opened his eyes and was once again back in the monastery. After that event, Father Melchizedek's life was transformed, for he had refocused his life on repentance and prayer, just as St Mary, through her sorrow, had urged him to do. Fr Tikhon explains this transformation in Fr Melchizedek . . .

> The fruits of his now exclusively spiritual labour were not delayed, revealing themselves in his deepest humility, his weeping over his past sins, his sincere love for all, and his complete and utter withdrawal from all affairs of this world.[4]

Father Melchizedek's vision was sharpened through the entrance of St Mary into his life. He saw that his high volume of productivity was actually getting in the way of what he had been called there to do: to enter into loving union with God and become a saint.

There is little for me to write after this story. What is there left to say? Is St Mary looking upon me in the same way? Is she watching me rush around and busy myself and yearn for writing, always slipping away to write somewhere, the desire to be adored and thought of as a great writer as part of my image, the mask I wear to somehow show that I exist. What is it all for? I can hear St Mary telling me, "All we wanted from you is to serve those around you in repentance and prayer." Repentance and prayer . . . Lord have mercy on us and save us.

22

THE SIMPLE WAY

HOW TO TRANSFORM THE STATE OF THE WORLD

In a world obsessed with complexity theory and 'global issues', there is a simple life, a simple Way, that opens to all of us if we seek it.

Behold, You desire truth in the inward parts, and in the hidden part You will make me to know wisdom. Psalm 51:6

Requisite Variety

About twenty years ago I fell in with a group of consultants. We worked with one of the most high profile think tanks in the world. A think tank that since Covid-19 has become almost a household name. Our work as consultants was informed by complexity theory: helping to create complex systems to overwhelm global problems and foster the emergence of other complex systems called 'the solution'. We were obsessed with complexity and systems theory. We advocated and practiced an orientation to the world that attempted to take complex problems and apply more complexity to them to overwhelm them and break them down into simple parts. We followed the Requisite Variety Principle from Stafford Beer's book *Designing Freedom*: that the variety of a problem can only be attenuated by bringing greater variety to its solution. We loved this stuff. We would sit for hours with other consultants and heads of state and Fortune 500 CEOs and movie actors and writers and talk about complexity. People loved it. People even just loved repeating the word, starting each sentence with it or embedding it endlessly in every phrase, it seemed, and drawing it out in the most pedantic and affected European accents that for the life of me I can't rid from memory: "Com-plex-ity …"

One year, just before I attended this conference in Switzerland, I read a quote by Jean Vanier that really impacted me. We were meeting up again as consultants to 'transform the world' by working with world leaders who'd taken up the global mandate to do so (whether anyone asked them to do so is besides the point!). But this quote by Jean Vanier really got me thinking: that the key is not to focus on transforming the world at all, but rather looking at the state of my own heart and beginning the transformation there. As one saint put it, "I'm going to transform the world—beginning with myself." How simple. Maybe too simple, I thought. Besides, what would such an orientation to all that complexity and systems talk look like? How would anyone get any real work done in the world!

The Simple Way

Two decades later, I find I'm changing: I'm desiring simplicity. There's something about the Way of Orthodoxy that can, over time, slim down one's focus and state of attention. Seen eucharistically, life becomes more one-pointed. Here's what I mean.

One day I was in confession going over the same list of passions as the week before. And my father of confession was doing the routine thing he does so well—he sits in silence and listens, then empathizes, then gives me something to think about before praying the prayer of absolution (sometimes he laughs his head off at my fumbling confession, but I'm not supposed to talk about that!).

"So this is it eh?" I asked breaking the silence after the prayer of absolution.

"What?"

"Well, I come to confession every week and list out my same passions, you listen, offer some points of reflection before praying the prayer of absolution."

"Yes."

"And then I go on my way and attend Diving Liturgy, struggle to say my morning prayers, go through the Wednesday and Friday fasts, and repeat the same cycle."

"Exactly."

"That's really simple, isn't it?"

"It is and it isn't, but yes—it's very simple."

"And little by little I heal a little more and a little more."

"Yes, pretty much—you'll take a couple of steps back from time to time, but that becomes the focus of spiritual life, those simple things . . ."

"I like it," I said after some time of being quiet and thinking.

"So do I."

The whole simplicity thing really struck me when I recently watched an interview with Father Paul Baba about his times spent with Father Seraphim Rose. I was particularly inspired by how often Fr Paul mentioned that Fr Seraphim prayed the Jesus Prayer. He said that Fr Seraphim would have a quick meal, then off he'd go because he needed to return to his hut to pray the Jesus Prayer—so simple. And those prayers, and the life he lived of simple abandonment to God, and the many liturgies he prayed, and the simplicity of his cassock and the board he slept on, and the little typewriter and candle lit icons—that simplicity brought him into the presence of God out of which he not only wrote wonderful books, and spoke searingly on the most controversial issues of his time, but he became the work of art God had intended him to become, namely a saint.

I think about that when I want to get all complicated about everything. When I stare at the prayer rope I passively wear around my wrist, I've been thinking lately about Fr Seraphim and his unflagging desire to get back to his hut to pray the Jesus Prayer. So simple.

Back to Creating Art

Andrei Tarkovsky is one of my favourite film producers. In fact, it's often that if I'm sitting down to seriously watch a film I get frustrated because I can't find anything good or interesting to watch. That's when I end up defaulting to Tarkovsky's *Stalker* or his epic film *Rublev*. Tarkovsky wrote a wonderful book on art and creativity—he had a lot to say about the creation of art. He understood his movies, his art, as not merely entertainment but as creating the occasion for people to see the enchanted world more vividly, to, as he put it, "make an impression … of being the cause of an emotional trauma . . . of winning people not by . . . rational argument but through the spiritual energy with which the artist has charged his work."[1] He says that the preparation for this kind of work, "the preparatory discipline it demands" is not a formal "scientific" or particularly 'technical' discipline, but rather "a particular spiritual lesson." To put it another way, it's not about complexity, but a kind of transcendent simplicity. Tarkovsky argues for a different Way of creating art, one that is born out of the spiritual life of the artist, and that this actually transcends technical or scientific skill. In fact, if you watch his movies, the protagonists are all like that: scientists struggling with transcendence, and artists struggling with the illusion of having to become more scientific.

For instance *Stalker* is about a place called The Zone: a place that was believed to have been inhabited by aliens who had since left. There is a part of The Zone that would reveal to the person who entered it their deepest desires. The one who took people to this part of The Zone was known as 'the Stalker'. In the movie, two of the three protagonists are a scientist and a writer. The third is the Stalker. When the Stalker takes them deep into The Zone and to the place where their deepest desires would be fulfilled, indeed to the place of the heart, the writer and scientist decline to enter in the end, much to the despair of the Stalker himself. The Stalker returns home, falls on the floor and cries aloud,

> They call themselves intellectuals! Scientists, artists! They don't believe in anything! . . . My God, what kind of people are they? The look of their eyes is blank. They're thinking of how not to sell themselves cheap, how to earn more, how to get paid for every breath they take. They know they were born to "be someone," to be

> special! They say, "You only live once." How can such people believe in anything at all?[2]

Tarkovsky's lamenting Stalker, a holy fool who stands alone in a fallen world offering people a chance to enter the heart, is contrasted and complimented in the director's other film *Rublev*. In *Rublev*, the bell maker is a boy who has no skill or training whatsoever, but through great faith and prayers performs the impossible. The artist must be that way; must flee the complex and learn to deal with the crushing humility of faith and simplicity.

> Art is [thus] born and takes hold wherever there is timeless and insatiable longing for the spiritual, for the ideal: that longing which draws people to art. Modern art has taken a wrong turn in abandoning the search for the meaning of existence in order to affirm the value of the individual for its own sake.[3]

Art is born out of the timeless and insatiable longing for the spiritual. St Silouan elaborates this point:

> Man discovers his real self at the deepest roots of his nature when mind and heart, turned towards Christ, are joined—not by his own efforts but by the action of God—in mystic union.[4]

This is the beginning of any work, of any transformative effort whether artistic or otherwise.

St Silouan again ...

> When the soul in the Holy Spirit comes to know the Lord, she never ceases to marvel at God's mercy, at His majesty and power, and the Lord Himself, of His grace,

> gently, like a mother with her beloved child, trains the soul to have good and humble thoughts, giving her to feel His presence and nearness, and the soul in humility contemplates the Lord and has no other thoughts.[5]

Our work, our lives, our art, showing love to those around us—thus taking part in transforming the world around us —is made up of simple elements: saying the Jesus Prayer, going to confession, receiving the Eucharist, all as often as possible. Struggling through the fast days and morning prayers, for He is the only one worth struggling for in a world that is ever passing away.

To transform the world is to enter into loving union with God. Only He can transform us more and more into Himself. And as we become more like Him we can be a loving and healing presence to those around us, indeed to a broken world. To begin is to enter the simple Way.

23
ONE WORD OF TRUTH
ALEXANDER SOLZHENITSYN AND THE COURAGE OF ART

In his Nobel Prize speech, Alexander Solzhenitsyn reveals the connection between Art and Courage, and the artist's responsibility to stand for Truth, Beauty, and Goodness.

Blessed are those who have regard for the weak; the Lord delivers them in times of trouble. The Lord protects and preservers them—they are counted among the blessed in the land—He does not give them over to the desire of their foes. Psalm 41:1

Men Have Forgotten God

If you haven't yet read Alexander Solzhenitsyn's *The Gulag Archipelago*, you should—especially in the times we're living in now, for it outlines in detail the savage and calculated brutality of the Stalinist Soviet Union that led to the death of sixty million Russians. What's shocking to read is the way the gulags crept up on an unwitting Russian populace. A man is walking to work one morning, a truck pulls up, the door opens, and the man is grabbed and thrown into the back among a pile of other people and transported away. Gone. No parting words to his wife or hugs and kisses from his children. Just simply taken off the street. The ones to go first were the journalists, academics, artists, and clergy. But there was nowhere to run or hide—for anyone. No one was safe from the gulag system of terror. The gulags were filled with political leaders and political pundits who had found themselves on the wrong side of Stalin's extemporaneous tyranny. And then there's Solzhenitsyn.

Solzhenitsyn was serving in the military in East Prussia in February 1945 when he was arrested and taken to the gulags. For what charge? Writing a personal letter to a friend in which he expressed disdain for how Stalin was handling the war and the need for a new organization to replace the Soviet regime. Solzhenitsyn was accused of spreading anti-Soviet propaganda and for "founding a hostile organization" and then taken to the Lubyanka prison in Moscow. He was finally sentenced to an eight-year term in a forced labour camp. It was a decade of imprisonment and exile that led him to embrace the Russian Orthodoxy of his childhood in a deeper way, and to share all he could about the gulags in which he witnessed such unspeakable suffering, torture, and death.

Solzhenitsyn saw the gulags and the mass systemic deaths of the Russian people to be the result of the "Dechristianization of Russian culture," which he considers the Bolshevik Revolution to be the culprit along with the great schism of the Russian Orthodox Church in 1666.

Solzhenitsyn writes,

> But if I were asked today to formulate as concisely as possible the main cause of the ruinous revolution that

> swallowed up some sixty-million of our people, I could not put it more accurately than to repeat: Men have forgotten God; that's why all this happened.

The Nobel Prize Lecture

In 1970, Solzhenitsyn was awarded the Nobel Prize in Literature for *The Gulag Archipelago*—a book that sold tens of millions of copies and had "amounted to a head-on challenge to the Soviet state." In his acceptance speech, Solzhenitsyn talked about the power of art to radically challenge tyrannical political systems, and to educate and inspire the masses to what is good, true, and beautiful.

For Solzhenitsyn, when it comes to art, we are like a "puzzled savage who has picked up a strange object cast from the ocean"—we don't know if it's been "unearthed from the sands" or "fallen down from the sky." We turn the object this way and that; we turn it over to discover not only what it is but what to do with it. But all we can do is discover some mundane function but never dreaming of its higher function.

So it is with art. Holding it in our hands, we "confidently consider ourselves to be its masters." We speak on its behalf, and attempt to somehow renew it. We monetize it, seek to profit from it, turn it into advertising or political propaganda for "narrow minded social ends." And in such cases, like the "puzzled savage" we can hardly dream of its higher purpose, even though "in each application it gives to us a part of its secret inner light. But shall we ever grasp the whole of this light? Who will dare to say that he has defined art, enumerated all its facets?"

Art is primordial. It transcends man. We can represent it, but cannot possibly possess it. Solzhenitsyn's aspersion of those who seek to monetize or profit from art sounds much like the Stalker's lament of those he sought to take into the Zone, those whose eyes are blank and who believe in nothing at all. But when we authentically participate in art, it gives us part of its secret inner light. But to what end? That remains the question. Solzhenitsyn continues: An artist . . .

> Recognizing a higher power above, gladly works as a humble apprentice beneath God's heaven . . . [Thus the] artist has merely to be more keenly aware than others of the harmony of the world, of the beauty and ugliness of the human contribution to it, and to communicate this acutely to his fellow man.

And if one thinks the artist's role ends there in this kind of blithe harmony with the world, Solzhenitsyn continues,

> And in misfortune, and even at the depths of existence —in destitution, in prison, in sickness—his sense of stable harmony never deserts him.

To see, to be open and sensitive to the harmony of the world, the beauty and ugliness of the human condition, then communicate it accurately to one's fellow human being—that is one of the roles of the artist. To affirm Beauty and meaning and the harmony of all creation.

Artistry is a Gift from Heaven

Artistry, according to Solzhenitsyn, is a gift from heaven—a gift we must realize, affirm, and understand. Indeed, this artistic gift to humankind goes way back to the first humans.

> Right back in the early morning twilights of mankind, we receive it from Hands which we were too slow to

> discern. And we were too slow to ask: For what purpose have we been given this gift? What are we to do with it?

There's a prophetic element to Solzhenitsyn's understanding of art. There is a deep sense of responsibility to point our fellow men to the Beauty and sheer ugliness of the human condition. Art is a gift to us from God—a gift we've been "too slow to discern." Therefore those "will always be mistaken who prophesy that art will disintegrate, that it will outlive its forms and die." Thus, we will all die at some point or another, but art will remain. And what about Beauty?

> One day Dostoevsky threw out the enigmatic remark: Beauty will save the world. What sort of statement is that? . . . When in bloodthirsty history did beauty ever save anyone from anything? There is however a certain peculiarity in the essence of beauty, a peculiarity in the status of art: namely, the confiding news of a true work of art is completely irrefutable and it forces even an opposing heart to surrender. In times when Truth and Goodness are crushed, chopped down, seemingly nullified, Beauty can soar to that same place and fulfill the work of all three! Art for times of tyranny and destruction.

Is this not one way we can say that Beauty will save the world? Far from a "careless phrase," it is a prophecy, but not just for the times of the Bolshevik Revolution of 1917, or those of Solzhenitsyn's *Gulag Archipelago*, but for our times today—these times of creeping tyranny, mass human experimentation, suicide, mass formation psychosis, manufactured economic crises, and the systematic dismantling of long-held democratic systems. "And in that case," Solzhenitsyn continues, "art, literature might really be able to help the world today . . ."

Within this world, therefore, there is a prophetic responsibility that writers have to point people to Beauty, Truth, and Goodness in times of systematic deception, and dull persistent evil. And Russian literature has long been familiar with the notions that a writer can do much within his society, and that it is his duty to do so. A calling away from the navel-gazing existential to the political and fraternal.

In the following statement, Solzhenitsyn is foresees our times in the most prescient way.

> Violence, less and less embarrassed by the limits imposed by the centuries of lawfulness, is brazenly and victoriously striding across the whole world, unconcerned that its infertility has been demonstrated and proved many times in history. What is more it is not simply crude power that triumphs abroad, but its exultant justification. The world is being inundated by the brazen condition that power can do anything, justice nothing.

The Dostoevsky of Our Times

I believe Solzhenitsyn is a prophet for our times as Dostoevsky was for the decades preceding the Bolshevik Revolution and the rise of Stalinism—indeed an epoch of tyranny, world war, unbridled chaos and death.

> Dostoevsky's *Devils* . . . are crawling across the whole world in front of our very eyes, infecting countries where they could not have dreamed of; and by means of the hijackings, kidnapping, explosions and fires of recent

> years they are announcing their determination to shake and destroy civilization!

Yes—today, the devils, the demons, of radicalism and tyranny are determined to shake and destroy civilization. Were you seeing this Alexander? Were you seeing these very times today when you gave this speech so many years ago? The brazen conviction that power can do absolutely anything. We are seeing a wickedness growing in our world that is systematic—a grand collusion against the human race that has been played out cosmically since the creation of man through the shedding of flesh and blood for Truth, Beauty, and Goodness, and continues today through mass manipulation, silencing of voices who cry out against injustice and bring corruption to light. And if you think I'm mincing words when I laud Solzhenitsyn for his prescience, just read this next statement and see for yourself!

> It would seem the appearance of the contemporary world rests solely in the hands of the scientists; all mankind's technical steps are determined by them. It would seem that it is precisely on the international goodwill of scientists, and not of politicians, that the direction of the world should depend. All the more so since the example of the few shows how much could be achieved were they all to pull together.

What we are seeing today is what can be accomplished when a small group of powerful people seek to control and subjugate and manipulate and use the entire human race. Political pundits, news agencies, health care officials, and entertainers, international financiers, private meetings in Swiss ski villages where the future of the world is literally designed and engineered without our knowledge or purview—the design and strategic implementation of the brave new world. "You will own nothing, have no privacy, and be happy." Corruption runs amok, and incense and libations are lavished upon the god 'Science', and everyone bows down to it and obeys its priests and gives their lives over to it for the pittance it gives back, namely a false sense of security that comes from compliance.

> And who, if not the writer, are to pass judgement—not only on their own unsuccessful governments . . . but also on their people themselves, in their cowardly humiliation or self-satisfied weakness? Who is to pass judgement on the lightweight sprinters of youth, and on the young pirates brandishing their knives.

Here Solzhenitsyn reveals an important role of the writer: to report on, expose, and indeed pass judgment on governments and those who abet them—the compliant ones who engage in what Hannah Arendt poignantly described as "the banality of evil". Who else is in a position to artistically expose the evil of one's times?

> We shall be told: what can literature possibly do against the ruthless onslaught of open violence? But let us not forget that violence does not live alone and is not capable of living alone; it is necessarily interwoven with falsehood. Violence finds its only refuge in falsehood, falsehood its only support in violence.

Violence and falsehood are logically interconnected, for "Any man who has once acclaimed violence as his method must inexorably choose falsehood as his principle." Tyranny and oppression are nourished by silence and complicity. Complicity is deceitful. In a world today drunk with cowardice, silence, and complacency, the words of Solzhenitsyn represents a calling to writers everywhere. And in revealing the responsibility of the writer to expose evil, he also reveals the key to writing, indeed to art itself.

> And the simple step of a simple courageous man is not to partake in falsehood, not to support false action! Let [the lie] enter the world, let it even reign in the world—but not with my help.

Writing and Spiritual Practice

Hence the act of art and writing is connected to spiritual practice—to affirm Beauty, Truth, and Goodness. Writing thus ought to be a spiritual exercise that comes out of the writer's own pursuit of Truth and Goodness, and the Beauty of the writer's heart as it is filled with God. In such a pursuit, art and prayer become united. The artist, the writer, seeks God first before any other inspiration or any other act. And the prayer that comes from the heart of the artist is to know the difference between what is true and what is false, what is real and what is fake. It is prayer ever upon the heart for the Holy Spirit to show me the truth and falsehood of a given situation—especially of my own fantasies and illusions—and then to embolden me to enter that situation, to choose the side of truth with courage and strength and wisdom.

Such a spiritual practice becomes a warfare within myself—not just externally in the world. I must hunt down the falsehood in my heart; all the ways I blithely profess or support or collaborate with falsehood that lead to unchecked compliance and cowardice. And such a way of living becomes a way of art, that is, what St Porphyrios calls living poetically. Living poetically is pursuing a life of prayer that seeks loving union with God and all creation in Love. The movement is internal, which then draws me into the world of others. St Porphyrios . . .

> You don't become holy by fighting evil. Let evil be. Look towards Christ and that will save you. What makes a person a saint is love.

Thus we can interpret Solzhenitsyn's words about art and the battle against falsehood spiritually. Not that we should not struggle against falsehood in the world, but that the struggle must always begin with ourselves through prayer and a life devoted to love.

> But writers can achieve more: they can conquer falsehood! In the struggle with falsehood art always did win and it always does win! Openly, irrefutably for everyone! Falsehood can hold out against much in this world, but not against art.

It is in the act of creating art that is true and good and beautiful that we strike out against, call out, and expose the systemic evil of our times. The work of the artist is thus the work of a prophet—it is a kind of prophecy: to be attuned to and expose the lies of our age and call out the workers of lawlessness. To not let silence set in on tyranny. But the movement, the direction of this artistic action always begins inward, and then moves outward in love: love for God, love for His world, and love for each human being we encounter—to see Christ in everyone.

One Word of Truth

For Solzhenitsyn, when falsehood is rejected, denied, not allowed to fester, then "the nakedness of violence will be revealed in all its ugliness—and violence, decrepit, will fall." And in such a time, the role of the writer is "to help the world in its white-hot hour" not by making excuses of powerlessness, or, God forbid, "by living a frivolous life—but by going to war!" Here is where art, writing, and ascesis meet. And following this part of Solzhenitsyn's speech is a line that should strike at the heart of all I do, written and unwritten; a line that should haunt me in my sleep, and terrify me when I am going about my day; a line that if I were to put into practice would change my life and the lives of others, and indeed the course of history:

> One word of truth shall outweigh the whole world.

Solzhenitsyn once wrote that his life changed when he made the decision that he was only going to speak and act based on what is true; that in all things he was going to work at shunning falsehood. How much of my life is a chimera so that others will like me? And if this desire to be admired dwells in my life, in my heart, how will it not seep out into my writing? How many of my decisions come from what looks good to others or presents a certain mask to the world?

I resonate with this one statement—an irony that comes out of psychoanalysis: I'm not what I think I am. I'm not what you think I am. Instead, I am what I think you think I am.

When will I stop the lies? When will I choose, like Solzhenitsyn, to struggle to affirm and hold to what is true? But I can't do it on my own. And I can't do it through the right 'reasoning' or 'method' or 'process'—it's never worked, and is the reason for this whole mess in the world in the first place. The right answer to the psychoanalytic question above is "I am who Christ thinks I am". I must pursue Truth, Beauty, Goodness Himself, the Logos

Himself. And that is how I take Solzhenitsyn's affirmation of the truth and transcend it. For to be human, to affirm truth and beauty, begins with recognizing not the shortfalls of others, but rather my own shortfalls, my weakness, the banality of evil that exists in me. Such a movement is described here by St Silouan the Athonite:

> The man who cries out against evil men, but does not pray for them, will never know the grace of God.

When I look at Solzhenitsyn's quote above, "One word of truth outweighs the world," that word of truth must be applied to me. It's how I shed the lies and deceit, the bandages of experiences and accolades that I've wrapped around myself. It's how I begin a journey, the Way, of healing from illness. It's how, getting back to Merton, I become a saint by becoming my true self.

24
THE MASK WITH A THOUSAND FACES
METAVERSE, ART, AND THE CREATIVE MIND

In the metaverse, the self is torn between two worlds. If art is created through a self that is authentic, where does that leave the avatar?

The Lord is their strength, and He is the saving refuge of His anointed. Save Your people, and bless Your inheritance; Shepherd them also, and bear them up forever. Psalm 28:8-9

What is the Metaverse

What are we doing when we seek an alternative reality? What do we really want? What are we looking for? True community? A place to be oneself—whatever that means. To be united with something bigger than we are? To be accepted? What is the metaverse anyway? A hazy concept that has a number of components most of which are still in infancy.

The gateway into the metaverse is Virtual Reality (VR). It's like a portal that takes you out of this world, the real world, and into the digital world. VR, and its siblings like

Augmented Reality (AR) and Extended Reality (ER) are still in their infancy, and thus as portals will be emerging into very powerful gateways into this universe of our own making. In ten years, alternative realities in digital form will 'be' just as 'real' as the real—or 'really real'—world. What are the unintended consequences? We don't know—and how many really care? Nevertheless, it's far too early to tell. But already pioneers of this technology like Jarod Lanier are telling people to quit social media because of how it impacts the brain and other aspects of health and well-being—something we didn't know when we all jumped onto X (then called Twitter) and Instagram with relish and awe.[1] Social media is considered Web 2.0—and now we are at the gates of Web 3.0 while being urged to quit the last iteration of the internet. That should give us pause. We need to be critical about Web 3.0, which is called by some 'the metaverse', and for others 'digital worlds'.

Time out of Time, Space out of Space

What is the metaverse? Good question. It's hard to tell exactly what it is right now because it's emergent. But for the sake of a semblance of clarity, here are a few lines from *The Metaverse Handbook: Innovating the Internet's Next Tectonic Shift*:

> [The] Metaverse is not a destination. The Metaverse is a movement—a movement toward the digital-first livelihood we've slowly been adopting year over year, app by app. The Metaverse becomes more real every time we replace a physical habit with a digital equivalent. We, the digital citizens of the Internet, are manifesting the Metaverse by trading time in the meat space (the physical world) for time online.[2]

This is an important point that gets into the emergent nature of this new world—a world created incrementally by our own actions online: the more time we spend in the metaverse, the more we actualize its emergence by reducing the amount of time we spend in the natural world. Thus, "[the] Metaverse is the moment in time where our digital life is worth more to us than our physical life."[3]

The more time and resources we put into the metaverse, the more value we place on it over against the natural world. We are saying that we prefer the digital world to the natural one. If the metaverse is a moniker for the digital world, think about how much of the material world is going digital. And where attention goes, energy follows, and the transition starts to take place. This has been happening for decades, and the technology is growing exponentially. Five to ten years from now books like *Ready Player One* will be an outdated reality.

Attention is a form of worship. We worship what we pay attention to, what we are present for valued over against what we are not paying attention to. Presence opens reality to us, or it is the way we open the world. By being more present to the digital world than the natural world, we are leaving the material world God created for us for a world we've created based on our whims and desires and passions. In the Christian faith, the natural world is created by God, not out of necessity, but out of love for us. The natural world God created for us to be present in, attuned to, as well as the stuff of worship—the way we offer thanksgiving back to Him in a relationship of mutual love. We worship God by ordering the stuff of the natural world. We worship God by offering what He has given us back to Him: water, smoke, wood, oil, wine, bread . . . For as we say in the Liturgy of St Basil, "We give thanks for what is Yours, for everything, concerning everything, and in everything."

However, we can put ourselves over against the natural world through our egos, i.e., by believing that we are nothing but the stuff of our thoughts, that is our thoughts are the ground of the natural world; that we posit the world through our thoughts and so on.

The Cartesian Theatre

What Descartes did in his philosophy was overturn the natural hierarchy of the world by placing the self, consciousness, thought, above God, i.e., by concluding that the presupposition of God is human thought, the human mind itself. How do I know that God is not deceiving me into believing that the natural world, and even I myself, exist? That was the pinnacle of Descartes' skepticism. He wanted to take skepticism to the very end and envisage some kind of evil deity that would deceive him into believing that he and the natural world existed. In such a situation, the only thing Descartes believed he could trust at that point was the fact that he was thinking. So according to Descartes, how do you know that some malicious deity isn't deceiving you? Because you are thinking; and if you are thinking, then you must exist as the agent of that thinking. And if you exist, and you are thinking about God, then He must somehow exist too.

Cartesian philosophy is one of the foundations of the metaverse. I become the true centre of my world. The world—my world—exists simply because I have posited it as such. My thinking opens the world to me. Is this not the metaverse, namely the extension of my own fluid thoughts and identity? We create a new world that is an extension of all of our fantasies; a place where our fantasies not only come true, but into which we can invite others.

In other words, the metaverse becomes a reality that is simply an extension of the passions.

Jared Lanier, pioneer of VR technology, describes the extended world of the passions very well in his book *Dawn of the New Everything: Encounters with Virtual Reality*. Lanier tells the story of how he came up with the concept of VR—or was inspired to its conclusion. He was in the library reading some books and papers on various technologies when he came across some writers about virtual reality. Suddenly he had an epiphany: Virtual Reality would be a place where one could make one's fantasies realized, and not only that but one would be able to share those fantasies with others. Your wildest imagination could be given a kind of verisimilitude that you could experience haptically—not only that, but you could then invite others to share those experiences with you.

> I was immediately obsessed with the potential for multiple people to share such a place, and to achieve a new type of consensus reality, and it seemed to me that a 'social version' of the virtual world would have to be called virtual reality. . . . I was fifteen years old and vibrating with excitement. I had to tell someone, anyone. I would find myself running out of the library doors so that I didn't have to keep quiet; rushing up to strangers on the sidewalk . . . "You have to look at this! We'll be able to put each other in dreams using computers! Anything you can imagine! It's not just going to be in our heads anymore![4]

From the words of the pioneer of VR himself, we can see that the metaverse is a theatre of your imagination that you can invite others into. You don't have to live solely in your head anymore, but you can share your fantasies with others and engage in them with them.

I am a Lama; Therefore I Exist

In the metaverse you can be whatever you want: human, animal, Ewok—anything. But the 'you' projected onto the metaverse is a 'you' that is reified through an avatar. It is a way of living with a divided self. Identity in the metaverse is fluid, malleable, multitudinous. In her book *The Future of You*, technologist Tracy Follows explains that what 'you' are in the metaverse will be multiple identities—in fact, as many 'yous' as you want.

In her article for *MIT Technology Review*, Taylor Fang suggests that she and other members of her generation are well-equipped to curate multi-faceted identities for themselves using the ever-increasing supply of social media tools. "To grow up with technology, as my generation has," she writes, "is to constantly question the self, to split into multiplicities, to try to obtain our own contradictions." But, for an increasing number of people, the question is not how best to harness social media to live our best lives, it is how to free ourselves from the constraints and expectations of real life by returning to the escapism of virtual worlds.[5]

Is not the authentic, the, as it were, 'good life' one that is lived in defiance of fantasies and imaginations? Don't the Church Fathers warn us about living in the imaginary, that we must cast off imaginations; that there is a vulnerability we open ourselves to when we live solely, and unnaturally, in our heads? And is not the metaverse simply an extension of our own heads, a way of forcing the brain to put connections together to deceive ourselves into believing that what we are experiencing is real? Is it not just one big fantasy?

One might object: what's wrong with living in a digital fantasy world? We've been watching television, writing fiction, making movies for decades and beyond—all to deliver fantasy to masses of people. What's wrong with making it more real and something we can share with people? It's fun and cool and useful in many different contexts, including work! Besides, one may continue to argue, the metaverse is less limited and more creative than the material world. For as we know, people act differently according to their avatar than they would in the material world. This difference in behaviour between the real and virtual world is called the Proteus Effect: the more attractive the avatar, the more willing the person is to approach strangers, for instance, and so on. Therefore, with my avatar I can live a completely different, freer life than I would in the material world. And think of all the excitement and pleasure!

If you want to go live in the metaverse, that's fine—it's your decision. But when it comes to creating art, engaging in creative life, becoming fully alive and fully who 'you' are, life in the metaverse will take you further away from what is real, including yourself. We are created for the material world and for relationship with God, others, and the created order. The life of the passions is the short-circuiting of those relationships to fulfill our own desires. And that short-circuiting leads to sickness and death.

Kevin Lee, head of China-based youth market consultancy Youthology:

> I have so many different selves, and they're all authentically me, but they're all different for different usages, different contexts, and different social circles.[6]

The fluidity of identity that the metaverse fosters thus raises a serious challenge to one wanting to become an authentic individual, an authentic person, which is the point of departure for art. When the metaverse is an extension of my imagination and myriad masks, then it becomes a place where I am encouraged to become less and less real. It becomes a place where who I would like to be supplants who I authentically am. The metaverse seems to be a breeding ground for glorified multiple personality disorder:

> If this trend continues, I think we will see our identities become more fluid than ever, as virtual media unlocks the possibilities of being who we would like to be, rather than settling for who we are. We will no longer seek merely to represent the self, but to invent the self, and to reinvent many selves that may co-exist in the various worlds we choose to inhabit.[7]

Follows concludes her book with the reflection that these multiple selves will eventually become extensions of who we are, and not merely second or third generation 'copies' of ourselves, copies of some 'core personality'. And what is the result of these copies of ourselves? To be "liberated of [our] physicality," and thus able to "revel in the freedom to express [ourselves]."[8] To be liberated from our bodies, which give us the "confidence," Fellows continues, "to unleash hidden talent" and become artists. The concern is that people are seeking to become authentic by rejecting their bodies which is the very thing that makes up the bulk of their identities.

We are embodied spirits. Our bodies are not mere 'shells' for our brains. And we are not just our brains either. There is no way, other than death, to liberate myself from my physicality. We are the physicality that we're made with in and of. Even the food we consume becomes part of us. What modern philosophy from Descartes on—and largely influenced by Plato—has done is attempt to disconnect the body from the mind. The body, according to Descartes and Spinoza (two pioneers of modern philosophy) was considered merely an 'extended thing'. David Hume, as much as he was an empiricist, claimed that when he tried to reflect on his own personhood—who he was—all he could see were his own thoughts and memories, but the body wasn't part of that identity.

From the modern period on, philosophy has been obsessed with the mind. If your body is simply something that you 'have' or 'carry around' with you, and not an important part of your being, of who you are, then you will be tempted to want to liberate yourself from it for a new digital extension of yourself. However, if indeed the body is a vital part of who you are, and not simply something you 'have' or merely carry around with you, then liberating yourself from your physicality to become 'yourself' is not a movement towards authenticity but conversely that towards becoming less and less real.

Creating, artistry, is a movement of authenticity, of becoming more real, which is a movement of vulnerability. Vulnerability is standing in the presence of who you are among other persons, and standing as yourself in all aspects of your being without the aid of masks to hide or cover the shortcomings you usually can't look at in yourself. By divesting the body from communication and life experiences, we are becoming more disembodied and thus less ourselves. To become an artist in such an environment is terrifying, because it is based on a whole slew of lies you need to tell yourself to make it somehow practical for you. But for many, being an artist is simply based on experience or having the right experiences—and the wilder the better, especially if those experiences give one the impression of being disembodied.

Where Everyone Knows Your Name

In the book *Ready Player One*, the protagonist has just 'returned' from a period of orgiastic pleasure. He reflects on all that he had witnessed, all that he had experienced, and with whom he had committed such acts. Then he reaches the painful conclusion: that at the end of the day, after all the virtual experiences—regardless of how 'real' they seemed at the time—he was just a depressed teenager sitting alone in his room escaping his pain through virtual sex. When verisimilitude becomes chimera. The need for community, for communion with the other, is not respited or quenched in a disembodied encounter. Real encounter with the other is through the body, not exempt from it. Even experiences considered 'spiritual' are embodied.

Consider again the observation by Pavel Florensky on the spiritual encounter through beholding the icon—which by the way requires standing physically in front of and seeing with ones eyes, and praying before with ones mouth, if only under the breath, or in silence of the real world surrounding one:

> An icon remembers its prototype. Thus in one beholder it will awaken in the bright clarities of his conscious mind a spiritual vision that matches directly the bright clarities of the icon; and the beholder's vision will be comparably clear and conscious.[9]

Doorway to the True Metaverse

Is not the iconostasis the true doorway to the metaverse, the Metaverse of the Real? The iconostasis opens one to the really Real, the truly virtual. The Oxford English Dictionary defines 'virtual' as "Possessed of certain physical virtues or powers; effective in respect of inherent qualities; capable of exerting influence by means of such qualities; capable of producing certain effects or results; effective, potent, powerful." Pavel Florensky reminds us of the power of the iconostasis, or any icon, to open us to what is transcendent and real:

> [The] icon . . . brings the thing seen into immediate felt experience. Thus at the highest flourishing of their prayers, the ancient ascetics found that their icons were not simply windows through which they could behold the holy countenances depicted on them, but were also doorways through which these countenances actually entered the empirical world. The saints came down from the icons to appear before those praying to them.[10]

Is not then the icon—through prayer, direct encounter, and the Divine Liturgy itself—the true portal to the heavenly, to one's true self, to true community? In such a place, we enter into the community with the clouds of witnesses, with the Holy Trinity, St Mary, the choir of the saints, the heavenly hosts of angels . . . and we enter this community as inauthentic broken selves but brought into the presence of our true humanity, our true selves.

In this sense, the authentic form of the metaverse is true prayer. Standing before the icon, a mirror opens to our true selves—the sinner and the saint.

> There is not the slightest question in such experiences that what is coming through the icon is merely the viewer's subjective invention, so indisputably objective is its impact upon the viewer, an impact equally physical and

> spiritual . . . [And] we can only describe experiences of seeing it as a beholding that ascends.[11]

And what do we see in this unfolding that ascends? . . .

The fires of our lusts and the emptiness of our earthly hungers simply and wholly cease; and we recognize the vision as something that, in essence, exceeds the empirical world, as something acting upon us from its own dominion.[12]

The Really Real

Is this not what everyone is seeking in the metaverse—really virtual seeking? To escape the emptiness of our earthly hungers, those things that drive us, that lie outside of our control. Do we not seek to escape into another reality and there find acceptance, love, an unlimited bliss—to ultimately escape the weight and 'kick back' of the material world? And is this not what we find when we stand before God, the saints, and the whole heavenly hosts amidst plumes of incense and the delight of timbrels? To partake of the Lord's Body and Blood and enter into heavenly loving union with Him and those who partake with us, and indeed the entirety of the Church including the assembly of the saints and the hosts of heaven, and yes the entire cosmos! There we find true community when we are united through the Eucharist and stand in heaven as the Church, the Body, of Christ.

The authentic, virtual, really real Metaverse is the realm of heaven we stand fully embodied in before the altar and the iconostasis, and God Himself, the Way Who is Christ, descends upon the altar and is embodied, incarnated, again for us to partake of—not in mere thought or idea or concept, but with our mouths. He becomes Bread and Wine for us to partake of Him in our bodies. He unites with us by becoming Food that nourishes not just our minds and hearts but also our bodies. We are not disembodied in this really Real Metaverse, but fully embodied, fully alive, fully connected.

> So what are we doing when we celebrate the Liturgy? We are having a reception, a supper. We invite as our fellow guests the saints of our Church; we invite our father who has fallen asleep; our grandfather, our great-grandfather, our loved ones who have left us; we invite the angels. And Christ Himself comes and provides his body and blood. And this is what it means when we say: "having commemorated all the saints, let us commit ourselves and one another, and all our life to Christ our God." Having welcomed all the saints into our midst, having implored them, and made them our helpers, we now give ourselves to Christ.[13]

Here is where we find our true identity, our true rest, our true community, our true love. As St Augustine so aptly put it: "Our hearts are restless till they find their rest in You." I used to think this was a statement about the eschaton that we would experience after the second coming of Christ. But now I understand it as the Eucharist—what we experience here and now whenever we encounter Christ through His greatest gift to us. The really real reality where we are united with God and He is united with us, and in and through which we become fully alive, fully complete, fully ourselves, and fully united with everyone and all creation.

AFTERWORD

> *You are fairer than the sons of men; Grace is poured upon Your lips; Therefore God has blessed You forever. Gird Your sword upon Your thigh, O Mighty One, With Your glory and Your majesty. Psalm 45:2-3*

As book titles happen to come to one's mind, the title of this book came to me one afternoon twelve years ago while I was on a walk. It was a time when I was in therapy, on antidepressants, and deeply confused and troubled. The book came to me while sitting at a bench gazing up at trees and wondering if things would actually become normal in my life again. The conversations with my therapist and readings at the time were about becoming me, an authentic human being. And one of the issues I was struggling with was how I could do that in a healthy way as a writer, and what creativity would look like apart from the promethean way I had been trained in. Thus my struggles and desire for healing and restoration came forth in a book idea—naturally—along with the title itself. The book would be about creativity and becoming a person. But at the time, as in most cases when I set down to write a book, I didn't know that it would take so long to complete. What I also didn't know at the time was that it wasn't the writing that would take so long, but rather getting to the place in my life where this book could actually be written. Another way of saying it is, it wasn't the creating but rather the *becoming* that spanned the twelve years since I first stumbled upon this title while sitting on that park bench.

Creativity as Magic

In a famous letter by J.R.R. Tolkien to Milton Waldman —the man who would be Tolkien's publisher at Collins of *The Lord of the Rings* and the *Simarilion*—he juxtaposes the Elves and Sauron in their use of art through magic. The Elves deploy art for its own sake, to create Beauty. Sauron and the enemy in general deploy art for power and domination. The Elves' "magic is Art, delivered from many of its human limitations: more effortless, more quick, more complete. And its object is Art, not power, sub-creation, not domination and tyrannous reforming of Creation."[1] The enemy conversely "is always 'naturally' concerned with sheer Domination, and so the Lord of magic and machines; but the problem: that this frightful evil can and does arise from an apparently good root, the desire to benefit the world and others . . . according to the benefactor's own plans—is a recurring motive."[2] To put it simply, the Elves represent what Fr John Zizioulas calls "Priests of Creation" for they are beings who offer the world back to God through art and the pursuit of Beauty. Evil—represented by Sauron, Orcs, and other despicable creatures—does not seek sub-creation with God but rather to possess, control, and dominate the natural order for its own ends. Both affirm the natural order of things and both apply the same magic, namely Art. However, one seeks Beauty for its own sake, the other uses Art for greater power, control, and possession. For Tolkien, evil is a consequence of men and Elves falling prey to a lust for power.

This distinction between creativity as Beauty versus a kind of magic for possession and control reveals two sides of my life prior to writing this book and upon writing it. I had fallen in with people who had very good intentions, who wanted to use creativity as a process for something they believed was good. But their thirst for power led them into the occult and the use of magic to possess and dominate others. For when seeking to transform the world and lead it into the new age and a new humanity, you simply use the best tools you have. But this way of magic had a cost —it required something of me, ultimately wanting my soul.

When I was baptized Orthodox, one of the highlights, as odd as it may sound, was turning to the west and renouncing Satan and all his ways and then turning to the east and affirming Christ my Saviour. For I had realized that my plunge into despair and death was the attempt of the enemy to dominate and destroy me. That is his desire for all humanity. Why? Because we bear the image of God —all of us. And he can't stand it. He can't defeat God, so he and his fallen angels go after us: marring, degrading, killing, drugging, entertaining, technologizing us. Thus by the time baptism rolled around, at the outset of the global hysteria that would be Covid-19, I was ready. Besides, I had been in the occult for almost a decade and didn't know what hooks were there. Nevertheless, I was done with all the baggage of my past, of all the trappings and hooks of the magic I was taught under the guise of 'creativity'. While planes were being rerouted and grocery stores cleared out and people were locking themselves in their houses in fear, I fled to and came under the safety and Beauty of the holy Orthodox Church. At holy Baptism I became a new being by dying and rising with Christ, my body was then consecrated with holy oil, after which I received the Body and Blood of Christ for the first time in my life. I had entered Beauty and Beauty had entered me.

A New Being

This change through the sacraments of holy Baptism, Chrismation, and the Eucharist is not conceptual, it is not merely 'symbolic' as 'symbol' is used today like the face of a mobile app or something. No. This change according to the Bible and the doctrines of the Orthodox Church is *ontological*, namely it is a change of one's actual *being*. It is not a change of accidents, like getting a hair cut or a nose job or something, but rather a change of one's *essence*. One dies, and rises again. One's body becomes sanctified. One partakes of the Divine Logos Himself—into one's body. And one is then placed on a path of becoming. Becoming what? Well, what I have been writing about: becoming the work of Art God has created us to become—in other words, becoming saints, divine beings, not through merit or through entitlement, but through adoption as sons of God.

Things take time . . . Baptism took nine years from the time of my original re-turning to Christ. And as a response all I wanted to do was enter more deeply into Beauty and Being, deeper into this new life in Christ the Logos. And this new life in the Church has anchored me as a human being, a husband, a father, and, among other things, a writer. After baptism, while my now father of confession was walking me to the change area where I would put on my white clothes, he said to me, "You have been given a treasure. Now the rest of your life will be unpacking its myriad gifts." I didn't really know what that meant, but over time I started catching glimpses of it. And those glimpses started connecting to other writers and saints who have had similar yet even greater glimpses. The collection of those glimpses were turned into the preceding little chapters on creativity and becoming.

Creativity and Becoming has come out of that journey along the Way. But this journey into Beauty and Being has led me to seeing glimmers of Beauty and desiring to see more. Thus the work of writing continues, and thus becoming more and more myself.

The writing has led me deeper into Beauty, which will be the forthcoming book in this series: entering deeper into Beauty Himself, and allowing Him to restore my eyes, my perceptions, to see His Image in everyone, everywhere, and in all things.

ACKNOWLEDGMENTS

A book may bear the sole name of an author, but it is in no wise an individual accomplishment. A simple moment of reflection will bring to mind a number of people who played a role of some sort in the creation of the book—and it is no different in the case of *Creativity and Becoming.* Here is a small list of people who over the years helped make this book possible.

The first is the one who wrote the Foreword and shares the dedication with my family, the poet Nicholas Samaras. Thank you Nick for inspiring the journey I've been on that led to *Creativity and Becoming*, as well as for your willingness to read the manuscript, provide feedback, and write the Foreword. Thanks also to Peter Gobran for your friendship, prayers, and for reading the manuscript and providing encouragement and feedback. Moreover, I would like to add Rolf Nolasco who twelve years ago was my therapist at a time when the title for this book came to my mind, and who provided moments for me to see my life, and creative life particularly, as a way of becoming myself. Tom Rudmik, my employer and friend at Master's Academy and College in Calgary, Alberta who has given me a lot of time and space to learn, practice, and design programming in creativity, and whose conversations have inspired me over many years. And to my brother Jason for our countless conversations over the years about art and creativity, philosophy, and overall life—mostly while Miles Davis has played in the background. Love and thanks to my mom, of blessed memory, and dad for always encouraging me to pursue what was in my heart to do.

Someone asked me once, "What do you need to create?" My answer was simple and without hesitation: to know I am loved and to be loved—by God, and by my wife and children. Thank you to my wife and children for bearing with me over the years, all the days and hours of reading and writing, and for loving me so much and bringing so much joy and Beauty into my life.

Glory to God for all things!

NOTES

EPIGRAPH

1. "This Akathist, the *Akathist of Thanksgiving*, was found among the effects of Protopresbyter Gregory Petrov upon his death in a prison camp in 1940. The title is from the words of Saint John Chrysostom as he was dying in exile. It is a song of praise from amidst the most terrible sufferings." St. Vladimir Parish, stvladimirpgh.org.

1. CREATING IN A SECULAR AGE

1. Frances Stonor Saunders, "The Lost Tribe of Russia. The Philosophy Steamer: Lenin and the Exile of the Intelligentsia," *Guardian Book Review*, (April 2006).
2. Saunders, "The Lost Tribe of Russia."
3. Saunders, "The Lost Tribe of Russia."
4. See for instance Bruce V. Folz, *The Noetics of Nature: Environmental Philosophy and the Holy Beauty of the Visible*, (Chicago: Fordham, 2013).
5. Ivan Ilyin, *Foundations of Christian Culture*, trans. Nicholas Kotar (Waystone Press, 2019), 1-2.
6. Ilyin, *Foundations*, 3.
7. Ilyin, *Foundations*, 16.
8. Mark 16:15 NKJV
9. Ilyin, *Foundations*, 33.
10. Ilyin, *Foundations*, 38.
11. Ilyin, *Foundations*, 35.

2. "TO THE LAST WORD!"

1. Solzhenitsyn can rant and rave too, but his voice tends to descend into whining, especially when writing about Japanese food. See Alexandr Solzhenitsyn, *Between Two Millstones Volume 2*, trans. Clare Kitson and Melanie Moore (Indiana: Notre Dame, 2020), 131.

3. FROM REGRET TO GRATITUDE

1. Henri Nouwen, *Spiritual Formation: Following the Movement of the Spirit*, (New York: Harper, 2010), 63-64.
2. Nouwen, *Spiritual Formation*, 64.
3. Nouwen, *Spiritual Formation*, 65.
4. Nouwen, *Spiritual Formation*, 67.
5. Nouwen, *Spiritual Formation*, 67.
6. Nouwen, *Spiritual Formation*, 68.
7. Ephesians 3:18-19, NKJV.

5. THE DESPAIRING ARTIST

1. Betsy Lerner, *The Forest for the Trees: An Editor's Advice to Writers*, (New York: Riverhead, 2001), 120.
2. William Faulkner certainly saw a deep spiritual side of Hemingway in *The Old Man and the Sea*, stating in his review in *Shenandoah*—a literary journal from Washington and Lee University—that "This time, [Hemingway] has discovered God, a Creator." Flannery O'Connor thought such a sentiment was "nice" as she conveyed Faulkner's review of Hemingway in a letter to some friends. See *Letters of Flannery O'Connor: The Habit of Being*, Ed. Sally Fitzgerald, (New York: FSG, 1979), 56.
3. But maybe that wouldn't have helped him, given that he was allegedly a spy for the CIA. His suicide may have been a deliberate exit strategy. See Reynolds, Nicholas, *Writer, Sailor, Soldier, Spy: Ernest Hemingway's Secret Adventures, 1935-1961*, (New York: Harper, 2017).

6. ART AND THE WAY OF SAINTHOOD

1. Thomas Merton, *New Seeds of Contemplation*, (New York: New Directions, 2007), 29.
2. Merton, *New Seeds*, 30-31.
3. Merton, *New Seeds*, 32.
4. Merton, *New Seeds*, 32.
5. Merton, *New Seeds*, 34.
6. Merton, *New Seeds*, 34.
7. Merton, *New Seeds*, 35.
8. Merton, *New Seeds*, 35.
9. Merton, *New Seeds*, 35-36.
10. Merton, *New Seeds*, 36.

7. ART AND TRUTH

1. Mother Maria of Normanby as quoted in Bishop Kallistos Ware, *The Orthodox Way*, (New York: St Vladimir's), 85.
2. James 1:23-25 NKJV

9. THE WAY, THE ART, OF LETTING GO

1. Saint Porphyrios, *Wounded by Love: The Life and the Wisdom of Saint Porphyrios*, Trans. Father John Raffan, (Evia Greece: Denise Harvey, 2014), 218.
2. Saint Porphyrios, *Wounded by Love*, 218.
3. Father Joseph Shryvers, *The Gift of Oneself: Surrendering Oneself to God as a Way of Life*, (Charlotte: Tan, 2008), 89-90.
4. Shryvers, *The Gift*, 89-90.
5. Shryvers, *The Gift* , 89-90.

10. ART AS SILENCE AND PRAYER

1. Sister Gabriela, *Seeking Perfection in the World of Art: The Artistic Path of Father Sophrony*, (England: Stavropegic Monastery, 2014), 77.
2. Sister Gabriela, *Seeking*, 79-80.
3. Sister Gabriela, *Seeking*, 84.
4. Sister Gabriela, *Seeking*, 84.
5. Sister Gabriela, *Seeking*, 80.

11. WRITING FOR THE APOCALYPSE

1. Ware, *Orthodox Way*, 7.
2. Hieromonk Damascene, *Father Seraphim Rose: His Life and Works*, (Platina: St Herman, 2003), 640.
3. Damascene, *Father Seraphim*, 640.
4. Damascene, *Father Seraphim*, 640-1.

12. ENTERING INTO BEAUTY

1. Thomas Fisch, ed., *Liturgy and Tradition: Theological Reflections of Alexander Schmemann*, "Theology and the Eucharist," (Yonkers: St Vladimir's, 1990), 78, 83.
2. Archimandrite Aimilianos, *The Church at Prayer*, (Alhambra: Sebastian, 2012), Kindle, 998.
3. Aimilianos, *The Church*, Kindle 1051.

4. Alexander Schmemann, *For the Life of the World: Sacraments and Orthodoxy*, (Crestwood: St Vladimir's, 2002), 14-15.
5. Aimilianos, *The Church*, Kindle 1098.
6. Aimilianos, *The Church*, Kindle 1098.

13. CENTRING THE HEART

1. Thomas Merton, *Dialogues with Silence.*

14. REFLECTING UNCREATED LIGHT

1. Lewis, C.S., *Christian Reflections*, "What is Christian Literature," ed., Walter Hooper, (Grand Rapids: Eerdmans, 1967), 25-36.
2. Brother Patrick Hart, ed., *The Literary Essays of Thomas Merton,* "Theology of Creativity," (New York: New Directions, 1981), 360.
3. Merton, *Literary Essays*, 361.
4. Humphrey Carpenter, *Inklings: C.S. Lewis, J.R.R. Tolkien, Charles Williams, and their Friends*, (New York: Ballantine, 1981), 62.
5. Carpenter, *Inklings*, 62.
6. Carpenter, *Inklings*, 62.
7. Carpenter, *Inklings*, 62.
8. Saint Porphyrios, *Wounded*, 218.

15. THE LIFE OF THE ARTIST

1. Pavel Florensky, *Iconostasis*, Trans. Donald Sheehan and Olga Andrejev, (Crestwood: St Valdimir's, 1996), 16.
2. Florensky, *Iconostasis*, 20-21.
3. Florensky, *Iconostasis*, 22.
4. Florensky, *Iconostasis*, 22.
5. Florensky, *Iconostasis*, 25.
6. Florensky, *Iconostasis*, 68.
7. Florensky, *Iconostasis*, 69.
8. Florensky, *Iconostasis*, 69.
9. Florensky, *Iconostasis*, 69.
10. Florensky, *Iconostasis*, 71-72.
11. Florensky, *Iconostasis*, 72.
12. Florensky, *Iconostasis*, 70.
13. Florensky, *Iconostasis*, 79.
14. Florensky, *Iconostasis*, 80.
15. Florensky, *Iconostasis*, 80.
16. Florensky, *Iconostasis*, 90.
17. Florensky, *Iconostasis*, 90.
18. Florensky, *Iconostasis*, 92.

17. LIVING POETICALLY

1. St Porphyrios, *Wounded*, 188.
2. Fr Lev Gilet, *In Thy Presence*, (Crestwood: St Vladimir's, 1977), 21-22.
3. Gilet, *Presence*, 21-22.
4. Gilet, *Presence*, 21-22.
5. Gilet, *Presence*, 21-22.
6. Fr Lev Gilet, *The Burning Bush*, (Spring eld: Templegate, 1994), 19-20.
7. St Porphyrios, *Wounded*, 218.
8. St Porphyrios, *Wounded*, 218.
9. St Porphyrios, *Wounded*, 218.
10. St Porphyrios, *Wounded*, 218.
11. St Porphyrios, *Wounded*, 218.
12. St Porphyrios, *Wounded*, 218-19.
13. St Porphyrios, *Wounded*, 218-19.

18. OPENING THE SOUL TO GOD

1. Czeslaw Milosz, *Selected and Last Poems: 1931-2004*, Trans. Anthony Milosz (New York: Harper), xix.
2. Milosz, *Selected and Last Poems*, 297.
3. Karl Ove Knausgård, *My Struggle, Book 2: A Man in Love*, Trans. Don Bartlett, (London: Harvill, 2013), 497.
4. Silvia Plath, *The Bell Jar*, (London: Heinemann, 1963), 69.
5. Ted Hughes, "The Art of Poetry," in *Paris Review Interviews, Volume 3*, Int. Drew Heinz, (New York: Picador, 2008), 287.
6. Hughes, *Paris*, 287.
7. Hughes, *Paris*, 287.
8. Edna H. Hong, and Howard V. Hong, *The Essential Kierkegaard*, (Princeton: Princeton, 2023), 8.
9. Søren Kierkegaard, *Either/Or, Part I*, Trans. Ed. Howard V. Hong and Edna H. Hong, (Princeton: Princeton, 1987), 460. Indeed one of the most painful and ironically humorous of Kierkegaard's observations.

20. IN SEARCH OF LOST TIME

1. Joseph Frank, *Dostoevsky: A Writer in His Time*, (Princeton: Princeton, 2009), 181.
2. Fyodor Dostoevsky, *The Brothers Karamazov*, Trans. Constance Garnett, (New York: Heritage, 1949), 244.
3. Hieromonk Damascene, *Father Seraphim Rose: His Life and Works*, (Platina: St Herman, 2003).

4. St John Climacus, *The Ladder of Divine Ascent*, Trans. Colm Luibheid and Norman Russell, (Ramsey: Paulus, 1982), 88-89.
5. Henri Nouwen, *Behold the Beauty of the Lord: Praying with Icons*, (Notre Dame: Ava Maria, 2007), 31-33.
6. Nouwen, *Behold*, 31.

21. WHAT IS THE MOST IMPORTANT THING?

1. Tikhon, *Everyday Saints and Other Stories*, Trans. Julian Henry Lowenfeld, (Dallas: Pokrov, 2011).
2. Tikon, *Saints*.
3. Tikon, *Saints*.
4. Tikhon, *Saints*.

22. THE SIMPLE WAY

1. Andrey Tarkovsky, *Sculpting in Time: The Great Russian Filmmaker Discusses His Art*, Trans. Kitty Hunter-Blair, (Austin: UTexas, 1987), 38.
2. Andrei Tarkovsky, *Stalker*, directed by Andrei Tarkovsky (Moscow: Mosfilm, 1979), film.
3. Tarkovsky, *Sculpting in Time*, 38.
4. Archimandrite Sophrony, *St Silouan the Athonite*, Trans. Rosemary Edmonds, (Crestwood: St Vladimir's, 1991).
5. Sophrony, *St Silouan*, 153.

24. THE MASK WITH A THOUSAND FACES

1. See Jarod Lanier, *Ten Arguments for Deleting Your Social Media Accounts Right Now*, (New York: Holt, 2018). The arguments are strong; nevertheless the book remains proof that arguments alone will not cause one to break with a serious addiction. Instead, I would look at Jean-Claude Larchet's *The New Media Epidemic: The Undermining of Society, Family, and Our Own Soul*, (Holy Trinity: New York, 2019).
2. QuHarrison Terry and Scott "DJ SKEE" Keeney, *The Metaverse Handbook: Innovating for the Internet's Next Tectonic Shift*, (New Jersey: Wiley, 2022), 20.
3. Terry and Keeney, *Metaverse*, 20.
4. Jared Lanier, *Dawn of the New Everything*, (New York: Holt, 2017).
5. Tracey Follows, T*he Future of You*, (London: Elliott & Thompson, 2021), 83.
6. Follows, T*he Future*, 90.

7. Follows, T*he Future*, 91.
8. Follows, T*he Future*, 89.
9. Florensky, *Iconostasis*, 71.
10. Florensky, *Iconostasis*, 71.
11. Florensky, *Iconostasis*, 72.
12. Florensky, *Iconostasis*, 72.
13. Aimilianos, *The Church*.

AFTERWORD

1. J.R.R. Tolkien, The *Simarilion*, 2nd edition, Ed., Christopher Tolkien, (New York: Del Rey, 2001), xvi-xvii.
2. Tolkien, *Silmarillion*, xvii.

ABOUT THE AUTHOR

Jeff Graham is the Publisher of Saint Patrick Press. He has published two novels, *Hunger Strike* and *Transition Diaries*. *Creativity and Becoming* is his first work of non-fiction. Jeff's background is in philosophy, which he studied at the University of Toronto as well as a brief stint at Stanford University. Jeff was baptized into the Holy Orthodox Church in 2020 on the Feast of St Patrick. As a writer he is interested in the intersection of existentialism, ontology, and Orthodoxy—how the challenges of 'the human condition' are taken up and transcended in the doctrines, traditions, and mystical spiritual life of the Orthodox Church. Jeff is married with three children and lives in Calgary, Alberta Canada.

Printed in Dunstable, United Kingdom

65869956R00150